KEBRA NAGAST

(The Glory of Kings)

"Declare ye among the nations,
and publish and set up a standard;
publish, and conceal not..."
Jeremiah 50:2

Haile Selassie I
(Last of the Solomonic Kings)

H.I.M. *Negusa Negast,* His Imperial Majesty Haile Selassie I (Power of the Holy Trinity) Emperor of Ethiopia, King of Kings, Lord of Lords, Conquering Lion of the Tribe of Judah, Elect of God, Light of the Universe – displaying here the mystical and metaphysical "Salutation of Peace" or the Sign of the Holy Trinity. The triangle pointing downwards is an esoteric symbol representing the material phase of the Seal of Solomon; the six-pointed star is also known as the Star of David.

A Modern Translation of the
KEBRA NAGAST
(The Glory of Kings)

The history of the departure of God and His Ark of the Covenant
from Jerusalem to Ethiopia, and the establishment of the
religion of the Hebrews and the Solomonic line of kings
in that previously pagan country.

Compiled, Edited and Translated by
MIGUEL F. BROOKS

The Red Sea Press, Inc.
Publishers & Distributors of Third World Books

11-D Princess Road   P. O. Box 48
Lawrenceville, NJ 08648   Asmara, ERITREA

The Red Sea Press, Inc.

Publishers & Distributors of Third World Books

11-D Princess Road   P. O. Box 48
Lawrenceville, NJ 08648   Asmara, ERITREA

Copyright © 1995, Miguel F. Brooks
First Red Sea Press, Inc. Edition, 1996
Second Printing, 1996

Cover Design: Carles J. Juzang
                Linda Nickens

ISBN: 1-56902-032-9   Cloth
        1-56902-033-7   Paper

DEDICATED

To the memory of the great Prophet, Visionary, Philosopher
and Liberator, The Rt Excellent Marcus Mosiah Garvey,
National Hero of Jamaica and eminent champion of the
Black Race, for he strove mightily that
every man's dignity be recognized.

One God, One Aim, One Destiny.

KEBRA NAGAST
(The Glory of Kings)

CONTENTS

	Page
Note from the Editor	xiii
Acknowledgements	xvii
Introduction	xix
Note on Biblical References	xxviii
English Language Versions of the Kebra Nagast	xxix
La Gloria de los Reyes	xxxi

Chapters of the KEBRA NAGAST

Part I   The Beginning 3

1.	Concerning the Glory of Kings	5
2.	The Greatness of Kings	5
3.	The Kingdom of Adam	6
4.	Concerning Envy	6
5.	The Kingdom of Seth	7
6.	The Sin of Cain	7
7.	Concerning Noah	8
8.	The Flood	8
9.	The Covenant of Noah	9
10.	Concerning Zion	9
11.	Declaration of the Patriarchs	10
12.	Canaan	11
13.	Abraham	11
14.	The Covenant of Abraham	12
15.	Isaac and Jacob	13
16.	Reuben	13
17.	The Glory of Zion	14
18.	The Division of the Earth	15

Part II   Solomon and Sheba 17

19. The Queen of the South 19
20. Tamrin the Merchant 19
21. The Return of Tamrin to Ethiopia 20
22. The Queen of Ethiopia prepares for her
    Journey to Jeruasalem 22
23. The Queen of Ethiopia comes to Solomon
    the King 23
24. The Conversation of Solomon with the
    Queen of Sheba....................................24
25. Solomon and the Workman 25
26. Solomon's Instructions to the Queen 27
27. The Seduction of the Queen of Sheba 29
28. Solomon's Oath to the Queen of Ethiopia 30
29. Solomon's Sign to the Queen of Ethiopia 33
30. The Queen brings forth her Son Bayna-Lehkem...........33
31. Bayna-Lehkem sets out for Jerusalem 34
32. Bayna-Lehkem arrives in Gaza 36
33. Solomon makes Bayna-Lehkem Captain
    of his Host..37
34. Solomon's Conversation with Bayna-Lehkem 40
35. Solomon questions his Son Bayna Lehkem...............42
36. Solomon sends Nobles of Israel to Ethiopia
    with his Son 44
37. Bayna-Lehkem (Menyelek I) is anointed
    King of Ethiopia, and is called David II 45
38. Zadok's commands to David II 46
39. The Blessing of Kings 47
40. The Ten Commandments 49

Part III   African Zion 53

41. The Priests and Officials of the Court of
    David II in Ethiopia 55
42. The King must not be reviled 57

43. The Conspiracy of the Sons of the Nobles
who are to go to Ethiopia 58
44. The plot to remove the Tabernacle of Zion
from the Temple in Jerusalem 60
45. The offering of Azariah and the King 61
46. How they removed the Tabernacle of Zion 62
47. How Solomon Blessed his son David II 63
48. The Farewell of David II; The Grief
of the People 64
49. David II (Menyelek I) receives the Covering
of the Tabernacle of Zion 65
50. The Gift of the Chariot of Zion to Ethiopia 67
51. How the People of Ethiopia Rejoiced 68
52. Zadok the Priest discovers that the
Tabernacle of Zion has disappeared 70
53. How Solomon rose up to slay them 72
54. Solomon arrives in Egypt 73
55. Solomon's Lament for the Tabernacle of Zion 74
56. Solomon's Return to Jerusalem 78
57. The Elders of Israel keep the Departure of
Zion a Secret 81

Part IV   The Fall of Israel 85

58. How the Daughter of Pharaoh seduced Solomon 87
59. The Sin of Solomon 88
60. Concerning the Prophecy of Christ 89
61. The Death-Lament of Solomon 90
62. The Pearl and the Saviour 93
63. The Conversation of Solomon with the Angel 96
64. The Reign of Rehoboam 97
65. Mary the Daughter of David 100
66. The King of Rome 100
67. The First Judgment of Adramis, King of Rome 103
68. The King of Medyam.......................................104
69. The King of Babylon 105

ix

70.	Concerning Lying Witnesses	105
71.	The King of Persia	110
72.	Concerning the King of Moab	111
73.	The King of Amalek, a Descendant of Lot	112
74.	The King of the Philistines	113
75.	How the Son of Samson slew the Son of the King of the Philistines	115
76.	Abraham's Journey into Egypt	116
77.	The King of Ethiopia Returns to his Country	119
78.	How Queen Makeda made her Son King of Ethiopia	121
79.	What ye shall eat: The Clean and the Unclean	123
80.	How the Kingdom of Bayna-Lehkem (David II, Menyelek I) was established in Ethiopia	124
81.	How the Men of Rome destroyed the Faith	125
82.	The First War of the King of Ethiopia	126
83.	How the Authority of Bayna-Lehkem was universally accepted	128

Part V   The Seed of the Woman 131

84.	The Prophecy about Christ	133
85.	The Murmuring of Israel	136
86.	The Rod of Moses and the Rod of Aaron	138
87.	Parable of the Two Slaves (The Devil and Adam)	143
88.	How the Angels rebelled against God when He created Adam	144
89.	Concerning Him that existeth in everything	149
90.	The Rejection of the Word	150
91.	The Horns of the Altar	152
92.	The Ark of Noah and the Talk of the Wicked	152
93.	The Belief of Abraham	154
94.	Prophecies Concerning the Coming of Christ	154
95.	Christ's Glorious Entrance into Jerusalem	160
96.	The Crucifixion	161

97.	The Resurrection	163
98.	The Ascension of Christ and His Second Coming	164
99.	The Prophets as Forerunners of Christ	165
100.	The Chariot and the Vanquisher of the Enemy	168
101.	The Return of Zion	170
102.	The Judgment of Israel	170
103.	The Chariot of Ethiopia	171
104.	The King of Rome and the King of Ethiopia	172

Appendix 1: Ethiopia (Abyssinia)
– A Brief Historical Synopsis 175

Appendix 2: The Falashas 179

Bibliography 187

List of Illustrations

1. Emperor Haile Selassie I
2. The Ark of the Covenant
3. Makeda, Queen of Sheba
4. Al-Aqsa Mosque (Dome of the Rock)
5. The Wailing Wall (Western Wall)
6. Rescue of the Ethiopian Jews
7. The Dominions of David and Solomon

Note from the Editor

This volume contains an English translation of the famous Ethiopian work, KEBRA NAGAST, The Glory of Kings. This book has been held in the highest honour in Ethiopia for several centuries and has been, and still is, venerated by the people as containing the final proof of their descent from the Hebrew Patriarchs, and of the kinship of their kings of the Solomonic line with Jesus Christ, the Son of God.

In other words, the book proves:

1. That the lawful kings of Ethiopia were descended from Solomon, King of Israel.

2. That the Tabernacle of the Law of God, the Ark of the Covenant, was brought from Jerusalem to Aksum by Menyelek, Solomon's firstborn son.

3. That the God of Israel transferred His place of abode on earth from Jerusalem to Aksum, the ecclesiastical capital of Ethiopia.

Menyelek was performing the Will of God in removing the Tabernacle of Zion from Jerusalem, as God was satisfied that the Jews were unworthy[1] to be custodians of the Ark wherein His Presence was[2], and the Ark wished to depart. Ethiopia had stretched out her hands to God (Psalm 68:31) and He went to her with the Ark, to preside over Menyelek's kingdom, which was established in accordance with the commandments that He had given Moses and the prophets and priests of Israel.

The line of kings founded by Solomon continued to reign even after the Ethiopians became Christians under the teaching of Frumentius and Adesius, and that line continued unbroken until the tenth century of our era. God then permitted the line to be separated from the throne, and allowed the Zagwe Kings to rule over Ethiopia until the reign of Yekuno Amlak, who restored the Solomonic dynasty A.D. in 1270.

Ethiopian literature documents a legend to the effect that when God made Adam He placed in his body a "Pearl" or " Seed"[3] which He

---

[1]Isaiah 65:1-7   [2]Kings 19:15   [3]I John 3:9

intended should pass from Adam into the bodies of a series of holy men, one after the other, until the appointed time when it should enter the body of Mary, and form the substance of her firstborn son Jesus, the Christ. This "Pearl" had passed through the body of Solomon, an ancestor of Jesus Christ. Jesus Christ and Menyelek, the son of Solomon by the Queen of Sheba, were sons of Solomon, and so, they were akin to each other. But Christ is the Son of God, and therefore, being the kinsman of Christ, Menyelek was divine.

The KEBRA NAGAST asserts that the kings of Ethiopia who were descended from Menyelek were of divine origin, and that their words and deeds were those of gods.

The Ark of the Law which Menyelek removed from the Temple of Jerusalem was a rectangular box made of hardwood plated with gold, and measuring about four feet long, two feet six inches wide, and two feet six inches deep. It was provided with a cover upon which rested the Mercy seat and figures of the Cherubim.[1] In the KEBRA NAGAST no mention is made of the Mercy seat and the Cherubim, but we read there that Moses made a case shaped like the "belly of a ship," and in this the Two Tables of the Law were placed. The case made by Moses carried the written Word in stone, and later on the Woman carried the living Word Incarnate. Although western history is silent as to the place where the Tabernacle of the Law was finally deposited, Ethiopian tradition asserts that it survived all the troubles and disasters that came upon the Abyssinians in their wars with the Muslims, and that it was preserved at Aksum.

This complete, modern translation of the KEBRA NAGAST derives mainly from the Spanish version of this work which appeared in Toledo in 1528 and in Barcelona in 1547, with its French version published in Paris in 1558. Many subsequent translations and editions have been made into German, English, Italian and other languages.

This popular edition conforms to the classic literary style of Budge' s Translation-Commentary, with its elegant Old English phraseology and syntax. After verifying and correlating its factual aspects with pre-

---

[1]Exodus 25:17-22

vious manuscripts and other reference sources, the editor proudly presents this new edition of the KEBRA NAGAST (The Glory of Kings) in order to establish the truth of the origins of the Solomonic dynasty of Kings and the current abode of the Ark of the Covenant.

Its companion manuscript, the FETHA NAGAST, or the book of the Justice of the Kings is currently being translated into Spanish and remains virtually unknown to the world, along with the vast collection of Ethiopian literature written in "Geez" the language of the Aksumite empire, precursor of modern Ethiopia.

The Editor

ACKNOWLEDGEMENTS

I wish to express my deep gratitude to the Embassy of Israel in Jamaica for the extraordinary assistance provided towards this project. The wealth of research material they gave me proved to be of invaluable help. I especially recognize the untiring support of Ambassador, H.E. Mr Uri Prosor; Cultural Attaché, Mr Abbie Avidan and Deputy Chief of Mission, Mrs Talya Lador-Fresher.

I am also greatly indebted to Mr Errol St B Smith, special consultant and principal contributor to this work, for providing rare comparative manuscripts and historical documents; to Mr M Matthews, Director, Press Department Embassy of Ethiopia, Washington, DC for his timely advice and assistance; to Prof. Beatriz Susana Bou, Department of Technical Translations, Universidad de Rosario, Argentina and Professors Linda Strebin and June Strebin of the Laboratorio de Idiomas, Universidad de Carabobo, Venezuela; who, as my former tutors, gave me valuable insight into the intricacies of ideological translation techniques.

Among those who helped edit and correct the original drafts, and who made many helpful manuscript suggestions are Mrs Deloris Williams and Miss Etta McLarty, both of Church Teachers' College, Mandeville; editor-researcher Mr Emerson F Dorway of West Indies College, and Pastor H H Holmes (Central Jamaica Conference of Seventh-Day Adventists). In manuscript review and final draft preparation, I had the expert assistance of Mrs Dorothea Oliphant-Watson, Mr Christopher Morrison and Miss Valerie Tibby.

Very gratefull thanks are due to the following institutions for providing research and reference materials: The World Jewish Bible Society, Israel Society for Biblical Research, The British Museum, El Archivo De Indias (Spain) and the Imperial Ethiopian World Federation.

Finally, my sincere thanks go to all those who offered words of encouragement and support, and to my family who patiently and stoically bore with me through these eight years of toil and labour.

INTRODUCTION

Ethiopia is a unique phenomenon in Africa for, along with Egypt, it is one of the two African nations that can trace its history into antiquity; but while Egypt became more and more alienated from its ancient culture owing to successive conquests, Ethiopia retained its original character, and has been able to preserve and to perfect an enduring culture born of the ancient encounter and the gradual fusion of two equally gifted peoples: the Cushites — who were most likely indigenous — and Semitic tribes who may have emigrated from Arabia.

The Egypt of the Pharaohs believed that it had received certain of its divinities from Ethiopia. The Greeks regarded it as the original home of wheat and of the olive tree; and recent anthropological discoveries confirm the antiquity of man's presence in Ethiopia.

Ethiopia has had a continuous existence as a nation for no less than 2,000 years, and for most of this period its contacts with the rest of the world were limited and intermittent.

The truly mystical and biblical era of Ethiopia's history began during the Sabaean period (around 750-650 BC) when there emerged on the Ethiopian plateau and coasts Sabaean influences from the south of Arabia. Among these were astral religion, sacred royalty and the language and writings that have been preserved by the Ethiopian church in the form of Geez (Ethiopic).

This Sabaean stage of its past led the Ethiopian nation to include in its ancient traditions the biblical episodes of the Queen of Sheba's visit to Solomon, as related in the First Book of Kings, Chapter 10:1-10. Then from the 2nd to the 9th centuries A.D. the mingling of new immigrants with people who had been on African soil for some time, created an independent nation based at Aksum on the plateau of the province of Tigre, and which still remains Ethiopia's religious centre.

The decline of the Aksumite empire began in the 7th century A.D. with the expansion of Christianity in the civilized world, which gravely affected the commercial revenues of these regions by devaluing incense and myrrh. At the same time, the Ethiopian Church retained an archaic Christianity that was very Semitic and still heavily influenced by the Judaism that had nurtured it. This, however, was balanced by the fact that Ethiopian emperors were considered the masters of the waters of the Nile river, which according to popular belief, they could divert to the point of starving Egypt.

During the 10th century, under very obscure circumstances, the usurping dynasty of the Zagwe kings appeared in Ethiopia, and later, ecclesiastical texts accused this dynasty of having not been of pure "Solomonic" stock, that is, not descended from the union of Solomon and the Queen of Sheba. The Zagwe, who were princes from the Lasta region of Central Ethiopia, took advantage of the eclipse of the Aksumite sovereigns to transfer the seat of the empire to their own region.

The restoration of the Solomonic dynasty of kings took place late in the 13th century when a powerful sector of the Church proclaimed the Solomonic princes to be the legitimate heirs of the Aksumite line, as defined by the traditions of the KEBRA NAGAST (The Glory of Kings). The Zagwe kings were suddenly swept away, and the restored Solomonic dynasty, starting with Yekuno Amlak (who ruled 1270-1285), transferred the seat of the empire further south to the province of Shoa.

The KEBRA NAGAST, or the Book of the Glory of Kings of Ethiopia, has been in existence for at least a thousand years, and contains the true history of the origin of the Solomonic line of kings in Ethiopia. It is regarded as the ultimate authority on the history of the conversion of the Ethiopians from the worship of the sun, moon, and stars to that of the Lord God of Israel.

It was during the era of the European conquests and colonization of the African continent, that renewed interest by scholars in the legendary country of "Prester Juan" began. Fragmentary accounts and oral reports of a remote Christian kingdom in the heart of Africa amidst a sea of pagan nations, captured the imagination of several European explorers. Both Spain and Portugal hoped to find in this kingdom a possible ally against Islam and the rising power of the Ottomans.

One of the earliest collections of documents of the country of the "Negus" (King) came through the writings of Francisco Alvarez, official envoy which Emanuel, King of Portugal, sent to David, King of Ethiopia, under Ambassador Don Roderigo De Lima. In the papers concerning this mission, Alvarez included an account of the King of Ethiopia, and a description in Portuguese of the habits of the Ethiopians, which was printed in 1533.

In the first quarter of the 16th century, PN Godinho published some traditions about King Solomon and his son Menyelek, derived from the KEBRA NAGAST. Further information about the contents of the KEBRA NAGAST was supplied by Baltazar Téllez (1595-1675),the author of the *Historia General de Etiopía Alta* (Coimbra, 1660). The sources of his work were the histories of Manuel Almeida, Alfonso Méndez and Jerónimo Lobo.

Among the most complete, and least known, translations of the KEBRA NAGAST, is the exhaustive work of Enrique Cornelio Agrippa (1486-1535) *Historia de las cosas de Etiopía* (Toledo, 1528) – a greatly amplified account. Agrippa was an alchemist, expert in magical sciences and Cabala, and physician to the King; he resided in the courts of Maximilian I and of Charles V; eventually he suffered imprisonment in Grenoble by orders of Francis I, where he died.

Additional information on Arabic additions to the original narratives of the KEBRA NAGAST was included by the Jesuit priest Manuel Almeida (1580-1646) in his *Historia de Etiopía* which does not appear to have been published in its entirety. Manuel Almeida was sent out as a missionary to Ethiopia, and had abundant opportunity to learn about the KEBRA NAGAST at first hand, owing to his excellent command of the language. His manuscript is a valuable work. His brother, Apollinare, also went out to the country as a missionary and was, along with his two companions, stoned to death in Tigre.

Job Ludof, whose *Historia Aethiopica* was published in Frankfurt in 1681, refers several times in his work to the *Historia General* by Baltazar Téllez, but it is pretty certain that he had no first-hand knowledge of the KEBRA NAGAST as a whole.

It was not until the close of the eighteenth century when James Bruce of Kinnaird (1730-1794), the famous British explorer, published an account of his travels in search of the sources of the Nile, that some information as to the fabulous contents of this extraordinary book came to be known among a select circle of scholars and theologians.

When he was leaving Gondar, Ras Michael, the powerful "Wazir" of King Takla Haymanot, gave him several most valuable Ethiopic manuscripts and among them was a copy of the KEBRA NAGAST. When the third edition of his *Travels in Search of the Sources of the Nile* was published, there appeared a description of the contents of the original manuscript. In due course these documents were given to the Bodleian Library at Oxford University.

In the year 1870 Francis Praetorious published, along with a Latin translation, the Ethiopic text of chapters 19 to 32 of the KEBRA NAGAST, edited from another manuscript by Domingo Lorda; this was given to the Bibliotheca Palatina. This work by Praetorious made known for the first time to the small circle of Western Ethiopic scholars, the exact form of the Ethiopian legend that makes the King of Ethiopia to be a descendant of Solomon, King of Israel, by Makeda, the Queen of Ethiopia, better known as the Queen of Sheba.

The beginnings of foreign penetration into Ethiopia followed the devastating Muslim attacks upon the kingdom in 1541. These were led by Ahmed Gran of Harar, causing the empire to appeal to Portugal for aid. Christopher da Gama, the son of Vasco da Gama, landed at Massaua in 1541 with 400 men, but was killed with most of his soldiers in a battle with the enemy. Subsequently a new army, equipped with firearms, was built up with the cooperation of the remaining Portuguese, and in 1543 Gran's forces were routed and their leader killed.

Attempts by the Portuguese who had assisted in the victory, and later by the Jesuits to convert the country to Roman Catholicism led to much conflict within the realm, until finally the Jesuits were expelled in 1633. Two centuries later, in 1855, Theodore, a military leader of vision, assumed the imperial title, and immediately began to revive the power of the empire and endeavoured to unite and reform the country.

However, as a consequence of the two-year delay by Queen Victoria of Great Britain, in replying to a letter Theodore had sent concerning the free use of the abundant annual flood waters of the Blue Nile, the Emperor imprisoned several British diplomats and officials at Magdala. All diplomatic efforts failed to secure their release, and in July 1867 a military force under Sir Robert Napier was dispatched to Ethiopia to secure the release of the British prisoners.

King Theodore and his army set out for Magdala to meet the British, but the mountain fortress was captured by Napier's forces in 1868, and Theodore committed suicide to avoid capture.

In August 1868, the great collection of Ethiopic manuscripts and documents that the British soldiers found at Magdala was taken away and brought to the British Museum. Among them were two fine copies of the legendary KEBRA NAGAST.

These manuscripts were classified as Oriental 818 and Oriental 819 respectively, and were fully described by Professor Wright in his *Catalogue of the Ethiopic Manuscripts* (London, 1877).

Within the context of the fascinating history of this fine manuscript of the KEBRA NAGAST (Oriental 819), written during the reign of Emperor Iyasu I (A.D.1682-1706), its eventual return to Abyssinia was truly providential, and it came about in the following manner: On the 10th of August, 1872, Prince Kasa, who was subsequently crowned as King John IV, wrote to the British nobleman Earl Granville, saying: "There is a book called KEBRA NAGAST which contains the law of the whole of Ethiopia, and the names of the Shums (Chiefs). I pray you find out who got this book, and send it to me, for in my country my people will not obey my orders without it."

A copy of this letter was sent to the British Museum and the trustees decided to grant King John's request. The manuscript was restored to him on 14th December 1872, with these words added to the last folio: "This volume was returned to the King of Ethiopia by order of the Trustees of the British Museum, December 14, 1872. (Signed) J. Winter Jones, Principal Librarian."

At the beginning of the 20th century, H Le Roux, an envoy from the President of the French Republic to Menyelek II, King of Ethiopia, went before the king, in order to see this manuscript (Oriental 819) and to obtain his permission to translate it into the French language. Le Roux, having made his request to Menyelek II personally, the king then made a reply, which LeRoux translates thus: "We are a people who defends itself not only by the force of arms, but also by the authority of its writings; and upon its traditions and history resides the strength of the kingdom. Myself as Emperor, and all subjects of the realm, agree that this book be translated into the French language, and thus bring to the knowledge of the peoples of the world that we are the custodians of God's Covenant through the treasures that he has bestowed upon us. By this it will be understood that God's aid shall always be with us, to deliver us from the enemies who attack us."

The king then gave orders that the manuscript was to be fetched from Addis Ababa, where the monks tried to keep it on the pretext of copying the text, and in less than a week it was placed in the hands of Le Roux, who could hardly believe his eyes.

Le Roux further commented: "I have achieved what I thought was impossible: the book which I now have in my hands contains the true history of the Queen of Sheba and of Solomon, the same that Negus and Priests of Ethiopia regard as the most authentic of all the versions that circulate within the European Libraries and among the Abyssinian monasteries. This is the book that King Theodore clutched against his heart on the night of his suicide; the same one that English soldiers carried away to London and which an ambassador returned to King John."

With the help of a friend, Le Roux translated several of the chapters of the KEBRA NAGAST, and in due course published his translation, *La Reine de Saba* (Paris, 1914).

The catalogues of the Ethiopic manuscripts in Oxford, London and Paris, which had been published by Dillman, Wright and Zotenberg, did supply a good deal of information about the contents of the KEBRA NAGAST in general, but scholars feel that it is impossible to judge the literary and historical value of the work by the mere transcription and translation of the headings of the chapters only.

In 1882, under the auspices of the Bavarian government in Munich, Germany, Dr C Bezold prepared an edition of the Ethiopic text edited from the best manuscripts available then, into a German translation, which was published under the aegis of the Bavarian Academy and entitled KEBRA NAGAST (Munich, 1909). The main authority for the Ethiopic text in Dr Bezold's edition is the famous manuscript which was sent as a gift to the Academie Française by King Sahla Dengel of Ethiopia, who died in 1855. According to Zotenberg in his *Catalogue des manuscrits ethiopiens* this manuscript must belong to the thirteenth century, and if this is so, then it probably is the oldest Ethiopic manuscript in existence.

None of the manuscripts of the KEBRA NAGAST give any indication as to the identity of its compilers, the time when it was written, nor the circumstances under which it was compiled. Most scholars do believe, however, that it was compiled soon after the restoration of the "Solomonic line of kings" when the throne of Ethiopia was occupied by Yekuno Amlak who reigned from 1270 to 1285.

It is possible that in its original form the Ethiopic text was translated from an Arabic version which in turn came from the Coptic since, during the one hundred and thirty-three years of the reign of the usurping Zagwe kings in Ethiopia (1137-1120), no one dared to compile the Solomonic traditions of the KEBRA NAGAST in any of the languages of the kingdom. Thus for the three centuries of the Zagwe era, it remained mainly in its Arabic version.

During the persecutions of the Christians in Egypt and in Ethiopia by the Muslims, in the tenth, eleventh and twelfth centuries, many churches, monasteries and their libraries of manuscripts perished. However, the Solomonic kings, who settled in the province of Shoa during the period of the Zagwe domination, managed to preserve chronological and genealogical records of their ancestry along with other historical documents that contained the annals of their predecessors.

The greater part of the narrative contained in the KEBRA NAGAST is based upon legends and traditions that are exceedingly ancient. These legends and traditions are derived from a variety of sources and can be traced to the Old Testament and Chaldean writings, also to Syrian works like the *Book of the Bee*, to ancient Khoranic stories and commentaries and to apocryphal books like *The Book of Adam and Eve, Kufale, The Instructions of Saint Peter to his disciple Clement, The Life of Hanna The Mother of the Virgin Mary, The Book of the Pearl,* and *The Ascension of Isaiah.* Along with extracts from these works, there are sections in which works attributed to Gregory Thaumaturgus and to Domitius, Patriarch of Constantinople, are quoted at length.

The purpose of the authors or compilers, and the later editors of the KEBRA NAGAST, remains a singularly inspired one: that is, to glorify Ethiopia by narrating the history of the coming of the "Spiritual and Heavenly Zion" — the Tabernacle of the Law of the God of Israel — of her own free will from Jerusalem to Ethiopia, and to make it quite clear that the King of Ethiopia was descended from Solomon, the son of David, King of Israel, and through him from Abraham and the early Patriarchs.

The KEBRA NAGAST was also intended to make the people of Ethiopia realize that their country was specially chosen by God to be the new home of the Spiritual and Heavenly Zion. This Zion existed originally in an immaterial form in heaven, where it was the habitation of God. When Solomon finished building the Temple of God, Zion was established there, in the Holy of Holies, and from it God made known His commands when He visited the Temple. It was at all times regarded to be the visible emblem of God Almighty and the material duplicate of the immaterial Zion in heaven.

It is hoped that in this brief introduction giving a sketch of the literary history of the KEBRA NAGAST, the reader will have found some useful insight into the majestic role that divine providence has set aside for the black race, and that in diligently reading with an open mind the dramatic unfolding of one of the most enigmatic and fascinating episodes in the continuing evolvement of God's relationship with man, further evidence of His infinite love towards us will be realized.

M F Brooks
1995

NOTE ON BIBLICAL REFERENCES

Biblical texts and references throughout the KEBRA NAGAST correspond to the rare Ethiopic Version, translated from the Septuagint in the 4th century A.D. This version of the Scriptures is thus around 1,200 years older than the "Authorised Version" (King James; 1611) and is by far, a more complete one.

ENGLISH LANGUAGE VERSIONS OF
THE KEBRA NAGAST

The existence of the KEBRA NAGAST seems to have been unknown in Europe until the middle of the 16th century, but the earliest English language summary of the contents of the KEBRA NAGAST was published by James Bruce of Kinnaird (1730-1794) in an account of his travels in search of the sources of the Nile river. Bruce had made for himself a copy of the KEBRA NAGAST which in due course he gave to the Bodleian Library, where they are classified as "Bruce 87" and "Bruce 93".

In 1877 Prof. W Wright of Cambridge University published a full *description* of the manuscript of the KEBRA NAGAST in the Makdala Collection at the British Museum. These are known as "variant readings" or scholarly commentaries supplied from Oriental manuscripts 818 and 819 now deposited at the British Museum.

In the year 1907 a rendering of the French version of the KEBRA NAGAST into English was made by Mrs J Van Vorst. This was entitled *Magda, Queen of Sheba* (New York, and London). However, as this version contains most of the legends and additions that were included in the Arabic language account, it is not regarded as an authoritative work.

The last known English translation-commentary on the KEBRA NAGAST was that done by E Budge, archaeologist, Egyptian and Assyrian antiquities (1857-1934) who conducted numerous excavations in Egypt and the Sudan. Budge's work is an extensive collation of Oriental 818 and Dr C Bezold's Bavarian Academy publication (1909). Both Bezold's text as well as the Oriental manuscript 818 represents the KEBRA NAGAST in the form that the Ethiopian priests and scribes have considered authoritative. Nevertheless, Prof. Wright had regarded these sources as "apocryphal works", and he thought it probable that an Arab author might have supplied the fundamental parts of the narrative, and that the authors of the Ethiopic version stated that the original source of their work was a Coptic archetype in order to give it an authority and importance which it would not otherwise possess.

It is believed that the Western Hemisphere division of the Ethiopian Orthodox Church has an abridged English language version of the KEBRA NAGAST, perhaps made by themselves from their own sources. In spite of several requests from this editor, however, I have not been able to peruse these.

It is important to note that virtually every English language translation and scholarly commentary of the KEBRA NAGAST, treats the work inclusive of all the legendary and obviously fictional stories, which are of undoubted Arabic sources, as one complete unit. No distinction is made between the original Geez writings and the later additions.

A careful study of the KEBRA NAGAST made while compiling and translating the work into English, has convinced me that the original form of the KEBRA NAGAST was that existing in the Coptic manuscript belonging to the Patriarchal Library at Alexandria, and that the Arabic version made from these was greatly supplemented by the scribes in the various monasteries of Egypt. Subsequently these enlarged versions found their way into Ethiopia via the Blue Nile.

This editor has received a French paraphrase of the Arabic text of the KEBRA NAGAST which was printed by Amelineau in his *Contes et Romans,* (Paris, 1888); also a copy in Spanish from the Arabic text printed by Bezold. From these I have been able to separate all the fictional additions, in order to bring out a complete and authentic version in English of the KEBRA NAGAST.

The extensive fictional and legendary narratives will appear in its entirety in a sequel to this modem version, and will be entitled, LEGENDS OF THE KEBRA NAGAST.

M F Brooks

La Gloria de los Reyes

Respecto de la Gloria Imperial

He aquí la interpretación elucidada de los Patriarcas respecto del esplendor, la grandeza y la dignidad que Dios otorgó a los descendientes de Adán, y muy especialmente concerniente al esplendor y la grandeza de Sión, el Tabernáculo de la Ley de Dios, del cual El mismo es el creador original, en su fortaleza sagrada, antes de la creación de ángeles y seres humanos. De ese modo el Padre, el Hijo y el Espíritu Santo en completa harmonía y total acuerdo, establecieron el Sión Celestial que sería la habitación de su gloria.

De tal fonna el Padre, el Hijo y el Espíritu Santo dieron la palabra, así: "Hagamos al hombre a nuestra imagen, conforme a nuestra semejanza"[1] y así en total acuerdo y voluntad opinaron ellos. Y el hijo pronunció, diciendo: "Yo encarnaré mediante el cuerpo de Adán," y el Espíritu Santo pronunció, diciendo: "Yo habitaré en el corazón de los Profetas y los Santos"; y este acuerdo y convenio se cumplió en Sión, la ciudad de su gloria.

Y así El crió a Adán en SU PROPIA IMAGEN Y SEMEJANZA, para de esta manera conquistar a Satanás el pecador orgulloso junto con sus seguidores, y establecer a Adán — su hijo propio — con los santos, con sus hijos, para su adoración. Ya que el portento de Dios fue concretado en sus palabras cuando El dijo: "Yo me haré hombre, y estaré en toda mi creación, en carne y hueso viviré." Y así en los dias postreros, por voluntad divina fue concebido en el cuerpo del Segundo Sión, el Segundo Adán, o sea nuestro Salvador, Jesucristo.

Esta es nuestra gloria y nuestra fé, nuestra esperanza y nuestra vida, el Segundo Sión.

---

[1]Genesis 1:26

Edited Spanish version of the KEBRA NAGAST
(Barcelona, 1547)
E C Agrippa; Manuel Almeida

KEBRA NAGAST
(The Glory of Kings)

PART I

The Beginning

"And the temple of God was opened in heaven, and there was seen in his temple the Ark of His Testament..."

Revelation 11:19

THE GLORY OF KINGS

1. CONCERNING THE GLORY OF KINGS

This is the interpretation and explanation of the Patriarchs concerning splendour, greatness and dignity, and how God gave them to the children of Adam, and especially concerning the splendour and greatness of Zion, the Tabernacle of the Law of God, of which He Himself is the maker and the fashioner, in the fortress of His Holiness before all created things, angels and men. For the Father and the Son, and the Holy Spirit with good fellowship and goodwill and cordial agreement together made the Heavenly Zion to be the place of habitation of their Glory.

Then the Father, and the Son, and the Holy Spirit said: "Let us make man in Our similitude and likeness" [1] and with ready agreement and goodwill They were all of this opinion. And the Son said: "I will put on the body of Adam," and the Holy Spirit said: "I will dwell in the hearts of the Prophets and the Righteous"; and this common agreement and covenant was fulfilled in Zion, the city of their Glory.

And He made Adam in *his own image and likeness*, so that He might remove Satan because of his pride, together with his host, and might establish Adam, His own plant, together with the righteous, His children, for His praises. For the plan of God was decided upon and decreed in that He said: "I will become man, and I will be in everything which I have created; I will abide in flesh." And in the days that came after, by His good pleasure there was born in the flesh of the Second Zion the Second Adam, who was our Saviour Christ. This is our Glory and our faith, our hope and our life, the Second Zion.

2. THE GREATNESS OF KINGS

Let us consider and let us begin to state which of the Kings of the earth, from the first even unto the last, in respect of the Law and the Ordinances and honour and greatness, we should magnify.

---

[1] Genesis 1:26

5

Gregory, the worker of wonders and miracles, who was cast into a cave because of his love for the martyrdom of Christ and suffered tribulation for fifteen years, said: "When I was in the pit I pondered over this matter, and over the folly of the Kings of Armenia, and I said, In what does the greatness of Kings consist?

Is it in the multitude of soldiers, or in the splendour of worldly possessions, or in extent of rule over cities and towns?" This was my thought each time in my prayer, and I was stirred to meditate again and again upon the greatness of Kings. And now I will begin.

3. THE KINGDOM OF ADAM

And I go up from Adam and I say, God is King in truth, and for Him praise is, and He appointed under Him Adam to be King over all that He had created. And he drove him out of the garden because of his apostasy through the sin of the Serpent and the plotting of the Devil. And at that sorrowful moment Cain was born, and when Adam saw that the face of Cain was ill-tempered and sullen and his appearance evil, he was sad. And then Abel was born, and when Adam saw that his appearance was good and his face good-tempered he said: "This is my son, the heir of my Kingdom."

4. CONCERNING ENVY

When they had grown up together, Satan had envy of him, and he cast this envy into the heart of Cain, who was envious of Abel first, because of the words of his father Adam, who said: "He who hath the good-tempered face shall be the heir of my kingdom"; and secondly, because of his sister with the beautiful face, who was born with him and who had been given unto Abel, even as God commanded them to multiply and fill the earth. The face of the sister who had been born with Abel resembled that of Cain, and their father had transferred the two sisters when giving them in marriage; and thirdly, because when the two brothers offered up sacrifice, God accepted the offering of Abel and rejected the

6

offering of Cain. Because of this envy Cain killed Abel. Thus fratricide was first created through Satan's envy of the children of Adam.

Having killed his brother, Cain fell into a state of trembling and panic, and he was repulsed by his father and His Lord. Then Seth was born, and Adam looked upon him and said: "Now hath God shown compassion upon me and He hath given unto me the light of my face. In sorrowful remembrance I will console myself with him. The name of him that shall slay my heir shall be blotted out, even to his ninth generation."

5. THE KINGDOM OF SETH

Adam died and Seth reigned in righteousness. And Seth died and Enos reigned, and Enos died and Cainan reigned. Then Cainan died and Mahalaleel reigned; Mahalaleel died and Jared reigned, and Jared died and Enoch reigned in righteousness, and he feared God, and God hid him so that he might not see death. And he became a king in his flesh in the land of the living. After Enoch disappeared Methuselah reigned, then Lamech reigned; and Lamech died and Noah reigned in righteousness and he pleased God in all his works.

6. THE SIN OF CAIN

That accursed man Cain, the murderer of his brother, multiplied evil and his seed did likewise, and they provoked God to wrath with their wickedness. They had not the fear of God before their eyes, and they never kept in mind that He had created them, and they never prayed to Him nor worshipped Him, nor called upon Him nor rendered service to Him in fear. They ate, drank and danced, and played upon stringed instruments and sang lewd songs; they worked uncleanness without law, without measure and without rule. And the wickedness of the children of Cain multiplied, until at length in their filthiness they introduced the seed of the ass into the mare, and the mule came into being, which God hath not commanded; even as those who give their children who are believers unto those who deny God, and their offspring become the seed of the filthy Gomorraites, one half of them being of good, and the other half of them of evil seed. As for those who do this wickedness, their judgment is ready and their error lasting.

7. CONCERNING NOAH

Noah was a righteous man. He feared God and kept the righteousness and the Law which his fathers had declared unto him (Noah was the tenth generation from Adam), and he kept in remembrance and did what was good. He preserved his body from fornication, and he admonished his children bidding them not to mingle with the children of Cain, the arrogant tyrant and divider of the kingdom who walked in the counsel of the devil, who maketh evil to flourish. Cain had taught them everything that God hated: pride, boastfulness of speech, self-adulation, calumniation, false accusation and the swearing of false oaths. And besides all these things, in the wickedness of their uncleanness, which was unlawful and against rule, man wrought pollution with man and woman worked with woman the abominable thing.[1]

8. THE FLOOD

This thing was evil before God, and he destroyed them with the waters of the flood which was colder than ice. He opened the doors of heaven and the cataracts of the flood poured down; He opened the fountains that were under the earth and the fountains of the flood appeared on the earth. The sinners were blotted out for they reaped the fruit of their punishment. And with them perished all beasts and creeping things, for they were all created for the glorification of Adam, and for his glory; some to provide him with food, some for his pleasure and some for the glorification of his creator so that he might know them, even as David said: "And Thou hast set everything under his feet"[2] for his sake they were created and for his sake they were destroyed, with the exception of eight souls, and seven of every kind of clean beasts and creeping things, and two of every kind of unclean beast and creeping things.

---

[1]Romans 1: 24-29   [2]Psalm 8:6

8

9. THE COVENANT OF NOAH

Noah the righteous man died and Shem reigned in wisdom and righteousness, for he was blessed by Noah when he said: "Be master to thy brother." And to Ham he said: "Be servant to thy brother." And he said unto Japhet: "Be thou servant to Shem my heir and be thou subject unto him."[1] And again after the flood, the Devil, our enemy, did not cease from his hostility against the children of Noah, but stirred up Canaan the son of Ham, and he became the violent tyrant and usurper who rent the kingdom from the children of Shem. They had divided the earth among them and Noah had made them swear by the name of his God that they would not encroach on each other's boundaries, and would not eat the beast that had died of itself or had been torn by wild animals, and that they would not cultivate harlotry against the law, lest God should again become angry with them and punish them with a flood.

As for Noah he humbled himself and offered up sacrifice, and he cried out and groaned and wept. And God held converse with Noah, who said unto him: "If Thou wilt destroy the earth a second time with a flood, blot Thou me out with those who are to perish." And God said unto him: "I will make a covenant with thee that thou shalt tell thy children that they shall not eat the beast that had died of itself or that hath been torn by wild beasts, and they shall not cultivate harlotry against the law; and I on my part, covenant that I will not destroy the earth a second time with a flood, and that I will give unto thy children Winter and Summer, Seedtime and Harvest, Autumn and Spring."[2]

10. CONCERNING ZION

"And I swear by Myself and by Zion, the Tabernacle of My Covenant, which I have created for a mercy seat and for the salvation of men, that in the latter days I will make it to come down to thy seed and that I will have pleasure in the offerings of thy children upon the earth, and the Tabernacle of My Covenant shall be with them forever. And whenever a cloud shall appear in the sky, so that they may not fear and imagine

---

[1]Genesis 9:25-27   [2]Genesis 8:21 and Genesis 9:4

9

that a flood is coming, I will make to come down from My habitation of Zion the Bow of My Covenant, that is the rainbow, which shall crown with colours the Tabernacle of My Law. And it shall come to pass that when their sins multiply and I am wishful to be angry with them, I will remember the Tabernacle of My Covenant, and I will set the rainbow in the sky, and I will put away Mine anger and will send compassion.

And I will not forget My Word, and that which hath gone forth from My mouth I will not take back. Though heaven and earth pass away My Word shall not pass away."[1] And the Patriarchs who were there answered and said to the blessed Gregory: "Behold now, we understand clearly that before every created thing, even the angels, and before the heavens and the earth, and before the pillars of heaven and the abysses of the sea, He created the Tabernacle of the Covenant, and that which is in heaven goeth about upon the earth."

11. DECLARATION OF THE PATRIARCHS

And they answered and said unto him: "Verily the Tabernacle of the covenant was the first thing to be created by Him, and there is no lie in thy word; it is true, correct, righteous and unalterable. He created Zion before everything else, to be the habitation of His glory, and the plan of His Covenant was that which He said: 'I will put on the flesh of Adam which is of the dust, and I will appear unto all those whom I have created with My hand and with My voice'." If the heavenly Zion had not put on the flesh of Adam, then God the Word would not have appeared and our salvation would not have taken place. The testimony is in the similarity ... the heavenly Zion is to be regarded as the similitude of the Mother of the Redeemer, Mary. For in the Zion which is built, there are deposited the Ten Commandments of the Law which were written by His hands, and He Himself, the Creator, dwelt in the womb of Mary, and through Him everything came into being.

---

[1] Matthew 24:35

12. CANAAN

It was Canaan[1] who rent the kingdom from the children of Shem, and he transgressed the oath which his father Noah had made them to swear. The sons of Canaan were seven mighty men, and he took seven mighty cities from the land of Shem and set his sons over them; likewise he also increased his portion double. And in later days God took vengeance upon the sons of Canaan, and made the sons of Shem to inherit their country. These are the nations they inherited: the Canaanites, the Perizzites, the Hivites, the Hittites, the Amorites, the Jebusites and the Girgasites; these are they whom Canaan seized by force from the seed of Shem. For it was not right for him to invade the Kingdom and to falsify the oath, and because of this they ceased to be and their memorial perished, through transgressing God's commandment and worshipping idols, and bowing down to them.

They are the ones who made magical images; they went to the tombs of their fathers and made an image or statue of gold, silver or brass, and a devil used to hold converse with them out of each of the images of their fathers, and say unto them: "My son, offer up unto me as a sacrifice the son whom thou lovest." And they slaughtered their sons and their daughters to the devils, and they poured out innocent blood to please filthy demons.

13. ABRAHAM

Terah begot a son and called him Abram, and when Abram was twelve years old his father Terah sent him to sell idols. And Abram said: "These are not gods that can deliver us," and he took away the idols to sell even as his father had commanded him. Then he said unto those unto whom he would sell them: "Do you wish to buy gods that cannot make deliverance, things made of wood, stone, iron and brass, which the hand of the artificer made?" And they refused to buy idols from Abram because of himself had defamed the images of his father. And as he was returning, he stepped aside from the road and he set the images

---

[1] Son of Ham (Genesis 10:6)

11

down, and looked at them, and said unto them: "I wonder now if you are able to do what I ask you at this moment, and whether you are able to give me bread to eat and water to drink?" None of them answered him since they were pieces of wood and stone; and he abused them and heaped revilings upon them and they never spoke a word. Then he buffeted the face of one, kicked another with his feet, and a third one he knocked over and broke to pieces with stones, and he said unto them: "If you are unable to deliver yourselves from him that buffeteth you, and you cannot repay with injury him that injureth you, how can ye be called 'gods'? Those who worship you do so in vain, and as for myself I utterly despise you, and you shall not be my gods." Then he turned his face to the east, stretched out his hands and said: "Be Thou my God, O Lord, Creator of the heavens and the earth, Creator of the sun and the moon, Creator of the sea and the dry land, Maker of the majesty of the heavens and the earth, and of that which is visible and that which is invisible; O Maker of the universe, be Thou my God. I place my trust in Thee, and from this day forth I will place my trust in no other save Thyself."

Then there appeared unto him a chariot of fire which blazed, and Abram was afraid and fell on his face on the ground; and God said unto him: "Fear thou not, stand upright." And he removed the fear from Him.

14. THE COVENANT OF ABRAHAM

And God held converse with Abram, and said unto him: "Fear thou not. From this day thou art My servant, and I will establish My Covenant with thee and with thy seed after thee, and I will multiply thy seed, and I will magnify thy name exceedingly. And I will bring down the Tabernacle of My Covenant upon the earth seven generations after thee, and it shall go round about with thy seed, and shall be salvation unto thy race; and afterwards I will send My Word for the salvation of Adam and his sons for ever.

Those who are of thy nation are evil men, and My divinity which is true, they have rejected. As for thee, that day by day they may not seduce thee, come get thee forth out of this land, the land of thy fathers, unto the

land which I will show thee, and I will give it unto thy seed after thee."
And Abram made obeisance to God and was subject to his God. And
God said unto him: "Thy name shall be Abraham;" and He gave him the
salutation of peace and went up into heaven.[1]

Abraham returned to his abode and he took Sarah his wife, and went
forth and did not go back to his father and his mother, nor to his house
and family. He forsook them all for God's sake. And he arrived in the
city of Salem, and dwelt there and reigned in righteousness, and did not
transgress the commandments of God. So God blessed him exceedingly, and at length he possessed three hundred and eighteen stalwart
servants who were trained in war, and who stood before him and performed his will. They wore tunics richly embroidered in gold, and they
had chains of gold about their necks, belts of gold round their loins and
they had crowns of gold on their heads; and by means of these men
Abraham vanquished his foes. He died in the glory of God, and was
more gracious and excellent that those who were before him. He was
gracious and held in honour, and highly esteemed.

15. ISAAC AND JACOB

Isaac his son became king and did not transgress the commandments of
God; he was pure in his soul and in his body, and he died in honour.
Then his son Jacob reigned, and he also did not transgress the commandments of God, and his possessions became numerous, and his
children were many; God blessed him and he died in honour.[2]

16. REUBEN

After him, Jacob's firstborn transgressed the commandments of God
and the kingdom departed from him and from his seed, because he had
defiled his father's wife, and his father cursed him and God was angry
with him. He became the least among his brethren, and his children
became leprous and scabby. Although he was the firstborn son of Jacob,

---

[1]Compare Genesis 12 and 13:14-17   [2]Genesis 35:9-12

13

the kingdom was rent from him.[1] Then his younger brother reigned and was called Judah because of this; his seed was blessed and his kingdom flourished. Ten generations after, Jesse reigned. And this is what I say concerning the kingdom: the blessing of the father was on the son, so that the kingdom was blessed with prosperity. As for the kingship over Israel, after the death of Jesse, David reigned in righteousness, in integrity, and in graciousness.

17. THE GLORY OF ZION

Concerning Zion, the Tabernacle of the Law of God; at the very beginning, as soon as God had established the heavens, He ordained that it should become the habitation of His glory upon the earth; and willing this He brought it down to the earth and permitted Moses to make a likeness of it. And He said unto him: "Make an ark or tabernacle of wood that cannot be eaten by worms, and overlay it with pure gold.[2] Thou shalt place therein the Word of the Law, which is the Covenant that I have written with my own fingers, that they may keep my law, the Two Tables of the Covenant."[3]

The heavenly and spiritual within it is of divers colours, and the work thereof is marvelous, resembling jasper and the sparkling stone, the topaz and the hyacinthine stone, and the crystal and light. It catches the eye by force and astonishes the mind and stupefies it with wonder. It was made by the mind of God and not by the hand of man. He himself created it for the habitation of His glory; it is a spiritual thing and is full of compassion; it is a heavenly thing and is full of light. It is a thing of freedom and a habitation of the Godhead, whose habitation is in heaven and whose place of movement is on earth. It dwelleth with men and with the angels; a city of salvation for men, and for the Holy Spirit a habitation.

Within it are a vessel of gold containing a measure of the manna which came down from heaven; the rod of Aaron which sprouted after it had become withered though no one watered it,[4] broken in two places it became three rods being originally only one rod.

---

[1]Genesis 35:22; Genesis 49:3-4; I Chronicles 5:1
[2]Hebrews 8:5   [3]Exodus 25:10   [4]Hebrews 9:4

Moses covered the Ark with pure gold and made for it poles to carry it, and rings in which to place them; and they carried it before the people until they brought it into the land of their inheritance. And prophets were appointed over the children of Israel in the Tabernacle of Testimony, and the priests wore the ephod[1] so that they might minister to the Tabernacle of Testimony; and the high priests made offerings so that they might obtain remission of their own sins and of the sins of the people likewise.

In this way did God command Moses on Mount Sinai, and He showed him the work and the construction and pattern of the Tent; and Zion was revered and had exceedingly great majesty in Israel, and it was acknowledged by God to be the habitation of His glory. He himself came down on the mountain of His holiness and He held converse with His chosen ones. He opened to them a way of salvation and He delivered them from the hand of their enemies. He spoke with them from the pillar of cloud and commanded them to keep His Law and His commandments, and to walk in the precepts of God.

This is the salvation of the children of Adam, for since the Tabernacle of the Law of God hath come down, they shall be called 'Men of the House of God' even as David said: "His habitation is in Zion.[2] And My habitation is here, for, I have chosen it; and I will bless her priests and make her poor to be glad. And unto David will I give seed in her, and upon the earth one who shall become king, and in the heavens one from his seed shall reign *in the flesh upon the throne of the Godhead.* As for his enemies, they shall be gathered together under his footstool, and they shall be sealed with his seal."

18. THE DIVISION OF THE EARTH

From the middle of Jerusalem, and from the north thereof to the southwest is the portion of the Emperor of Rome; and from the middle of Jerusalem from the north thereof to the south and to Western India is the

---

[1]Ephod: a sacred vestment worn by the high priest
[2]Psalm 9:11

15

portion of the Emperor of Ethiopia. For both of them are of the seed of Shem, the son of Noah, the seed of Abraham, the seed of David, the children of Solomon. For God gave unto the seed of Shem glory because of the blessing of their father Noah. The Emperor of Rome is the son of Solomon, and the Emperor of Ethiopia is the first-born and the eldest son of Solomon.

PART II

Solomon And Sheba

"I am black, but comely, O ye daughters of Jerusalem,
as the tents of Kedar, as the curtains of Solomon."

The Song of Solomon 1:5

19. THE QUEEN OF THE SOUTH

Our Lord Jesus Christ, in condemning the Jewish people who lived at that time, spoke saying: "The Queen of the South shall rise up on the Day of Judgment and shall dispute with, and condemn, and overcome this generation who would not hearken unto the preaching of My word, for she came from the ends of the earth to hear the wisdom of Solomon."[1] The Queen of the South of whom He spoke was the Queen of Ethiopia. And this Queen of the South was very beautiful in face, and her stature was superb. Her understanding and intelligence which God had given her were of such high character that she went to Jerusalem to hear the wisdom of Solomon. This was done by the Will of God and it was His good pleasure. Moreover, she was exceedingly rich, for God had given her glory, riches, gold and silver and splendid apparel, camels, slaves and trading men. And they carried on her business and traded for her by land, in India and in Aswan.

20. TAMRIN THE MERCHANT

There was a certain wise man, the leader of a merchant's caravan, whose name was Tamrin, and he used to load 520 camels and he possessed about 73 ships.

In those days King Solomon wanted to build the House of God, and he sent out messages among all the merchants in the east and in the west, in the north and in the south, bidding the merchants to come and take gold and silver from him, so that he might take from them whatsoever was necessary for the work. And certain men reported to him concerning this rich Ethiopian merchant, and Solomon sent to him a message and told him to bring whatsoever he wished from the country of Arabia; red gold, and black wood that could not be eaten by worms, and sapphires. That merchant was Tamrin, the merchant of the Queen of Ethiopia, and he went to Solomon the King, and Solomon took whatsoever he desired from him, and he gave to the merchant whatsoever he wished for in great abundance. Tamrin was a man of great understanding and he saw

---

[1]Matthew 12:42

19

and comprehended the wisdom of Solomon, and he marvelled and watched carefully so that he might learn how the king gave answers by his word, and understand his judgment and the readiness of his mouth, the discreetness of his speech and the manner of his life, also his occupations and his love, his administration and his table and his law. Those to whom Solomon had to give orders he addressed with humility and graciousness, and when they had committed a fault he admonished them gently. For he ordered his house in the wisdom and fear of God, and he smiled graciously on the fools and set them on the right road, and he dealt gently with the maidservants. He opened his mouth in parables and his words were sweeter than the purest honey. His whole behaviour was admirable and his whole aspect pleasant. For wisdom is beloved by men of understanding, and is rejected by fools.

When that merchant had seen all these things he was astonished and he marvelled exceedingly. Those who were accustomed to see Solomon held him in complete affection, and he became their teacher; and because of his excellence and wisdom those who had once come to him did not wish to leave him and go away from him.

The sweetness of his words was like water to the man who is thirsty, and like bread to the hungry man; like healing to the sick and garments to the naked man. He was like a father to the orphans, and he judged with righteousness and impartiality. He had glory and riches which God had given unto him in great abundance, namely, gold, silver, precious stones and rich apparel, cattle, sheep and goats innumerable. In the days of Solomon the King, gold was as common as bronze, and silver as lead; bronze, lead and iron were as abundant as the grass of the fields. God had given unto him glory, riches and wisdom, and grace in such abundance that there was none like unto him among his predecessors and among those who came after him.

21. THE RETURN OF TAMRIN TO ETHIOPIA

And it came to pass that the merchant Tamrin wished to return to his own country, and he went to Solomon and bowed low before him, embraced him and said unto him: "Peace be to thy majesty! Send me away and let me depart to my country, and to my Lady, for I have tarried long in beholding thy glory and thy wisdom, and the abundance of dainty meats which thou hast given me. And now I would depart to my Lady. If only I could abide with thee, even as one of the very least of thy servants, for blessed are they who hear thy voice and perform thy commands. If only I could abide here and never leave thee, but thou must send me away to my Lady because of what hath been committed to my charge, so that I may give unto her her property, for I am her servant." And Solomon went into his palace and gave unto him whatever valuable thing he desired for the country of Ethiopia, and he sent him away in peace. Tamrin then bade him farewell and went forth, journeyed along his road and came to his Lady, and delivered to her all the possessions which he had brought.

He related unto her how he had arrived in the country of Judah and Jerusalem, and how he had gone into the presence of Solomon the King, and all that he had heard and seen. He told her how Solomon administered justice and how he spoke with authority and decided rightly in all matters which he enquired into; how he returned soft and gracious answers, and how there was nothing false about him. He further related unto her how he appointed inspectors over the 700 woodmen who hauled the timber and the 800 masons who hewed the stone, also how he sought to learn from all the merchants and dealers concerning their craft and their country, and how he received information and imparted it twofold, and how all his handicraft and his works were performed with wisdom.

Each morning Tamrin related to the Queen about the wisdom of Solomon and how he taught wisdom and how he directed the affairs of the kingdom based on a wise system. For no man defrauded another nor stole the property of his neighbour, nor was there a thief nor a robber in his days. In his wisdom he knew those who had done wrong and he chastised them and made them afraid, and they did not repeat their evil deeds, but they lived in a state of peace and fear of the king.

These things did Tamrin relate unto the Queen, and each morning he recalled the things that he had seen with the king and described them unto her. The Queen was dumbstruck with wonder at the things that she heard from the merchant, her servant, and she pondered in her heart that she would go to Solomon the King; and she wept because of her great pleasure in those things that Tamrin had told her. She was most anxious to go to him, but when she considered the long journey she thought that it was too far and too difficult to undertake. Time after time she asked Tamrin questions about Solomon, and time after time Tamrin told her about him and she became most desirous to go that she might hear his wisdom, and see his face, and embrace him and petition his royalty. And her heart inclined to go to him, *for God had made her heart to desire it.*

22. THE QUEEN OF ETHIOPIA PREPARES FOR HER JOURNEY TO JERUSALEM

And the Queen said unto her subjects: "Ye who are my people, listen to my words for I desire wisdom and my heart seeketh to find understanding. I am smitten with the love of wisdom, for wisdom is far better than treasures of gold and silver, and wisdom is the best of everything that hath been created on the earth. Unto what under the heavens shall wisdom be compared? It is sweeter than honey and it makes one to rejoice more than wine; it shines more than the sun and it is beloved more than precious stones. It fattens more than oil, and it satisfies more than dainty meats, and it gives more fame than thousands of gold and silver. It is a source of joy for the heart, a bright and shining light for the eyes and a giver of speed to the feet; a shield for the breast and a helmet for the head.

It maketh the ears to hear and hearts to understand, it is a teacher of those who are learned, and it is a consoler of those who are discreet and prudent. It giveth fame to those who seek after it. And as for a kingdom, it cannot stand without wisdom, and riches cannot be preserved without wisdom; the foot cannot keep the place where it has set itself without wisdom. And without wisdom that which the tongue speaks is not acceptable. Wisdom is the best of all treasures. He who heaps up gold and silver does so to no profit without wisdom, but he who heaps up wisdom no man can snatch it from his heart. That which fools heap up, the wise consume. And because of the wickedness of those who do evil, the righteous are praised; and because of the wicked acts of fools the wise are beloved. So I will follow the footprints of wisdom and it shall protect me for ever." Then the Queen made ready to set out on her journey with great pomp and majesty, and with great equipment and many preparations. By the will of God her heart desired to go to Jerusalem so that she might hear the wisdom of Solomon, so then, she made ready to set out. Seven hundred and ninety-seven camels, and mules and asses innumerable were loaded, and she set out on her journey and travelled on without pause, and her heart had confidence in God.

23. THE QUEEN OF ETHIOPIA COMES TO SOLOMON THE KING

And she arrived in Jerusalem, and brought to the King many precious gifts which he desired to possess greatly. And he paid her great honour and rejoiced, and he gave her an habitation in the royal palace near him. He sent her food both for the morning and evening meal, each time fifteen measures of finely ground white meal, cooked with oil and gravy and sauce in abundance, and thirty measures of crushed white meal wherefrom bread for three hundred and fifty people was made, with the necessary platters and trays; ten stalled oxen, five bulls and fifty sheep without counting the kids, and deer, gazelles and fatted fowls, and a vessel of wine containing sixty measures, and thirty measures of old wine, and twenty-five singing men and twenty-five singing women, and the finest honey and rich sweets and some of the food which he himself ate, and some of the wine whereof he drank. And every day he arrayed her in eleven garments which bewitched the eyes. And he visited her and was gratified, and she saw his wisdom, his just judgments, his splendour, and his grace, and heard the eloquence of his speech. She marvelled in her heart and was utterly astonished in her mind, and she recognized in her understanding and perceived very clearly with her eyes how admirable he was. She wondered exceedingly because of what she saw and heard with him: how perfect he was in composure and wise in understanding, pleasant in graciousness and commanding in stature. She observed the subtlety of his voice and the discreet utterance of his lips, and that he gave his commands with dignity, and that his replies were made quietly and with the fear of God. All these things she saw, and she was astonished at the abundance of his wisdom, and there was nothing whatsoever wanting in his word and speech, but everything that he spoke was perfect.

Solomon was then working at the building of the temple of God, and he rose up and went to the right and to the left, and forward and backward. And he showed the workmen the measurement and weight and the space covered by the materials, and he told the workers in metal how to use the hammer, the drill and the chisel, and he showed the stonemasons the angle, the circle and the surface. And everything was done by his order, and there was none who set himself in opposition to his word; for the light of his heart was like a lamp in the darkness, and his wisdom was abundant as the sand. And of the speech of the beasts and the birds there was nothing hidden from him, and he forced the devils to obey him by his wisdom. And he did everything by means of the skill which God gave him when he made supplication to him; for he did not ask for victory over his enemies, and he did not ask for riches and fame, but he asked God to give him wisdom and understanding whereby he may rule his people, and build His house, and beautify the work of God and all that He had given him in wisdom and understanding.

24. THE CONVERSATION OF SOLOMON WITH THE QUEEN OF ETHIOPIA

Queen Makeda spake unto King Solomon, saying: "Blessed art thou, my Lord, in that such wisdom and understanding have been given unto thee. For myself I only wish that I could be one of the least of thine handmaidens, so that I could wash thy feet, hearken to thy wisdom, apprehend thy understanding, serve thy majesty and enjoy thy wisdom. O how greatly have pleased me thy answering, and the sweetness of thy voice, and the beauty of thy going, and the graciousness of thy words, and the readiness thereof. The sweetness of thy voice maketh the heart to rejoice, and maketh the bones fat, and giveth courage to hearts, and goodwill and grace to the lips. I look upon thee and I see that thy wisdom is immeasurable and thine understanding inexhaustible, and that it is like unto a lamp in the darkness. I give thanks unto Him that brought me hither and showed thee to me, and made me to walk upon the threshold of thy gate, and made me to hear thy voice."

King Solomon answered and said unto her: "Wisdom and understanding spring from thee thyself. As for me, I only possess them in the measure in which the God of Israel hath given them to me because I asked and entreated them from him. And thou, although thou dost not know the God of Israel, hast this wisdom which thou hast made to grow in thy heart, and it hath made thee come to see me, the vassal and slave of my God, and the building of His sanctuary which I am establishing, and wherein I serve and move round about my Lady, the Tabernacle of the Law of the God of Israel, the holy and heavenly Zion. I am the slave of my God and not a free man; I do not serve according to my own will but according to His will. And this speech of mine springeth not from myself, but I give utterance only to what He maketh me to utter. Being only dust He hath made me flesh, and from being only water He hath made me a solid man, and from being only an ejected drop upon the ground that would have dried up, He hath fashioned me in His own likeness and hath made me in his own image."

25. SOLOMON AND THE WORKMAN

And as Solomon was talking in this wise with the Queen, he saw a certain labourer carrying a stone upon his head and a leather-bag of water upon his neck and shoulders, and his food and his sandals were tied around his loins, and there were pieces of wood in his hands; his garments were ragged and tattered, the sweat fell in drops from his face, and water from the bag of water dripped down upon his feet. And the labourer passed before Solomon and as he was going by, the King said unto him: "Stand still!" and the labourer stood still. And the King turned to the Queen and said unto her: "Look at this man. Wherein am I superior to this man? And in what way am I better than this man? And wherein shall I glory over this man? For I am a man, dust and ashes who tomorrow will become worms and corruption, and yet at this moment I appear like one who will never die. Who would make any complaint against God if He were to give unto this man as He hath given to me, and if He were to make me even as this man is? Are we not both men? As is his death, so is my death; and as is his life so is my life. Yet this man is stronger to work than I am, for God giveth power to those who are feeble just as it pleaseth Him to do." Then Solomon said to the labourer: "Get thee to thy work."

And he spoke further unto the Queen, saying: "What is the use of us, the children of men, if we do not exercise kindness and love upon earth? Are we not all nothingness, mere grass of the field, which dries up in its season and is burnt in the fire? On earth we provide ourselves with dainty meats, and we wear costly apparel, but even whilst we are alive we are stinking corruption; we provide ourselves with sweet scents and delicate ointments, but even whilst we are alive we are dead in sin and in transgression; being wise, we become fools through disobedience and deeds of iniquity; being held in honour, we become contemptible through magic, sorcery and the worship of idols.

But the man who is a being of honour, who was created in the image of God, if he doeth that which is good becometh like God; and the man who is worth nothing, if he commiteth sin becometh like unto the Devil, the arrogant Devil who refused to obey the commands of His creator, and all the arrogant among men walk in his way, and they shall be judged with him. And God loveth the meek, and those who practise humility walk in His way, and they shall rejoice in His kingdom. Blessed is the man who knoweth wisdom, compassion, and the fear of God."

When the Queen heard this she said: "How thy voice doth please me! And how greatly do thy works and the utterance of thy mouth delight me! Tell me now: who is it right for me to worship? We worship the sun as our fathers have taught us to do, because we say that the sun is the king of the gods; and there are others among our subjects who worship other things; some worship stones, wood, trees; some worship carved figures, and some worship images of gold and silver. We worship the sun for he cooketh our food, and moreover he lights up the darkness and removeth fear; we call him 'Our King', and we call him 'Our Creator,' and we worship him as our God; for no man hath told us that besides him there is another god. But we have heard that there is with Israel another God whom we do not know, and men hath told us that He hath sent down to you from heaven a Tabernacle and hath given unto you a Tablet of the ordering of the angels by the hand of Moses the Prophet.

This also we have heard, that He himself cometh down to you and talketh to you, and informeth you concerning His ordinance and commandments."

26. SOLOMON'S INSTRUCTIONS TO THE QUEEN

And the King answered and said unto her: "Verily, it is right that men should worship God, Who created the universe, the heavens and the earth, the sea and dry land, the sun and the moon, the stars and the brilliant bodies of the heavens, the trees and the stones, the beasts and the feathered fowl, the good and the evil. Him alone we should worship in fear and trembling, with joy and gladness. For He is the Lord of the universe, the Creator of angels and men. It is He Who killeth and maketh to live, Who inflicteth punishment and showeth compassion, Who raiseth up from the ground him that is in misery, Who exalteth the poor from the dust, Who maketh to be sorrowful and Who maketh to rejoice, Who raiseth up and Who bringeth down. No one can rebuke Him, for He is the Lord of the universe, and there is no one who can say unto Him: 'What hast thou done?' And unto Him it is right that there should be praise and thanksgiving from angels and men. And verily there hath been given unto us the Tabernacle of the God of Israel, which was created before all creation by His glorious counsel. And He hath made to come down to us His commandments, done in writing so that we may know His decrees and the judgments that He hath ordained in the mountain of His holiness."

And the Queen said: "From this moment I will not worship the sun, but will worship the Creator of the sun, the God of Israel. And that Tabernacle of the God of Israel shall be unto me My Lady, and unto my seed after me, and unto all my kingdoms that are under my dominion. And because of this I have found favour before thee, and before the God of Israel my Creator, who hath brought me unto thee, hath made me to hear thy voice, hath shown me thy face and hath made me to understand thy commandments." Then she returned to her quarters.

The Queen used to go to Solomon and return continually, and listened to his wisdom, and kept it in her heart. And Solomon used to go and visit

27

her, and answer all the questions which she put to him, and he informed her concerning every matter that she wished to enquire about. After she had dwelt there six months the Queen wished to return to her own country, and she sent a message to Solomon, saying: "I desire greatly to dwell with thee, but now, for the sake of all my people I wish to return to my own country. As for that which I have heard, may God make it to bear fruit in my heart, and in the hearts of all those who have heard it with me. For the ear could never be filled with the hearing of thy wisdom, and the eye could never be filled with the sight of thy perfections."

It was not only the Queen who came to hear the wisdom of Solomon. Many used to come from cities and country, both from near and from far; for in those days there was no man found to be like unto him for wisdom (and it was not only human beings who came to him, but the wild animals and the birds used to come to him and hearkened unto his voice, and held converse with him), and then they returned to their own country, and everyone of them was astonished at his wisdom, and marvelled at what he had seen and heard.

When the Queen sent her message to Solomon, saying that she was about to depart to her own country, he pondered in his heart and said: "A woman of such splendid beauty hath come to me from the ends of the earth! What do I know? Will God give me seed in her?" And as it is said in the Book of Kings, Solomon the King was a lover of women.[1] And he married wives of the Hebrews, the Egyptians, the Caananites, the Edomites, the Moabites and from Rif[2] and Kuerge, Damascus and Syria, and women who were reported to be beautiful. And he had 400 queens and 600 concubines. This which he did was not for the sake of fornication but as a result of the wise intent that God had given unto him, and his remembering what God had said unto Abraham: "I will make thy seed like the stars of heaven for number, and like the sand of the sea."[3] And Solomon said in his heart: "What do I know? Perhaps God will give me men-children from each one of these women." Therefore when he did thus he acted wisely saying: "My children shall inherit the cities of the enemy, and shall destroy those who worship idols."

---

[1] I Kings 11:1   [2] Upper Egypt   [3] Genesis 22:17

These early peoples lived under the Law of the Flesh, for the grace of the Holy Spirit had not been given unto them. And to those who lived after Christ, it was given to live with one woman under the law of marriage. As concerning Solomon, no law had been laid down for him in respect of women, and no blame can be imputed to him in respect of marrying many wives. But for those who believe, the law and the command have been given that they shall not marry many wives, even as Paul said: "Those who marry many wives seek their own punishment. He who marries one wife hath no sin". And the law restraineth us from the sister-in-law in respect of the bearing of children.

27. THE SEDUCTION OF THE QUEEN OF SHEBA

King Solomon sent a message unto the Queen, saying: "Now that thou hast come here, why will thou go away without seeing the administration of the kingdom, and how the meals for the chosen ones of the kingdom are eaten after the manner of the righteous, and how the people are driven away after the manner of sinners? From the sight of it thou wouldst acquire wisdom. Follow me now and seat thyself in my splendour in the tent and I will complete thy instruction, and thou shalt learn the administration of my kingdom; for thou lovest wisdom and she shall dwell with thee until thine end forever."

The Queen sent a reply message, saying: "From being a fool I have become wise by following thy wisdom, and from being a thing rejected by the God of Israel I have become a chosen woman because of this faith which is in my heart; and henceforth I will worship no other God except Him. And as concerning that which thou sayest, that thou wishest to increase in me wisdom and honour, I will come to thee according to thy desire." And Solomon rejoiced because of this message, and he arrayed his chosen ones in splendid apparel, and he added a double supply to his table. He had all the arrangements concerning the management of his house carefully ordered, since the house of King Solomon was made ready for guests daily.

Then he ordered the royal table according to the law of the kingdom. And the Queen came and went into a place set apart in splendour and glory, and she sat down directly behind him where she could see and learn everything. And she marvelled exceedingly at what she saw and heard, and she praised the God of Israel in her heart. She was struck with wonder at the splendour of the royal palace which she saw, for she could see though no one could see her, even as Solomon had arranged in his wisdom for her. He had beautified the place where she was seated and had spread over it purple hangings and laid down carpets, and decorated it with marbles and precious stones; then he burned aromatic powders and sprinkled oil of myrrh and cassia round about, and scattered frankincense and costly incense in all directions. When they brought the Queen into this abode, the scent all round was very pleasing to her, and even before she ate the dainty meats therein she was satisfied with the smell of them.

With wise intent Solomon sent to her meats which would make her thirsty and drinks that were mingled with vinegar, and fish and dishes made with pepper; and he gave them to the Queen to eat. The royal meal had come to an end, and the administrators, the counsellors, the young men and the servants had departed, and the King rose up and he went to the Queen, and he said unto her: "Take thine ease for love's sake until daybreak." And she said unto him: "Swear to me by thy God, the God of Israel, that thou wilt not take me by force. For if I, who according to the law of men am a virgin, be seduced, I would then travel on my journey back in sorrow, affliction and tribulation."

28. SOLOMON'S OATH TO THE QUEEN OF ETHIOPIA

Solomon answered and said unto her: "I swear unto thee that I will not take thee by force, but thou must also swear unto me that thou wilt not take by force anything that is in my house." The Queen laughed and said unto him: "Being a wise man why dost thou speak as a fool? Shall I steal anything, or shall I carry out of the house of the King that which the King hath not given to me? Do not imagine that I have come here through love of riches. Moreover, my own kingdom is as wealthy as thine, and there is nothing which I wish for that I lack. Surely I have only come in quest of thy wisdom." And he said unto her: "If thou wouldst make me swear, swear thou to me also that neither of us may be unjustly treated." And she said unto him: " Swear to me that thou wilt not take me by force, and I on my part will swear not to take by force thy possessions." And he swore to her and made her swear also. And the King went up on his bed on one side of the chamber and the servants made ready for her a bed on the other side. Then Solomon said unto a young manservant: "Wash out the bowl and set in it a vessel of water whilst the Queen is looking on, and shut the doors and go and sleep." And Solomon spoke to the servant in another tongue which the Queen did not understand, and he did as the King commanded and went to sleep.

The King had not as yet fallen asleep, but he only pretended to be asleep and he was watching the Queen intently. The Queen slept a little and when she woke up her mouth was dry with thirst, for the food which Solomon had given her in his wisdom had made her thirsty indeed. Her mouth was dry and she moved her lips and sucked with her mouth but found no moisture. Then she determined to drink the water which she had seen, and she looked at King Solomon and watched him carefully; she thought he was sleeping a sound sleep. But he was not asleep; he was waiting until she should rise up to steal the water to quench her thirst. She rose up, and making no sound with her feet, she went to the water in the bowl and lifted up the jar to drink the water. But Solomon seized her hand before she could drink the water, and said unto her: "Why hast thou broken the oath that thou wouldst not take by force anything that is in my house?" And she answered and said unto him in fear: "Is the oath broken by my drinking water?" And the King said unto her: "Is there anything that thou hast seen under the heavens that is more precious than water?" And the Queen said: "I have sinned against myself and thou art free from thy oath. But let me drink water for my thirst." Then Solomon said unto her: "Am I then free from the oath which thou hast made me swear?" And the Queen said: "Be free from thy oath, only let me drink water." And he permitted her to drink water, and after she had drunk water he worked his will with her and they slept together.

Immediately after he slept there appeared unto King Solomon in a dream a brilliant sun, and it came down from heaven and shed exceedingly great splendour over Israel. And when it had tarried there for a

31

time it suddenly withdrew itself, *and it flew away to the country of Ethiopia, and it shone there with exceedingly great brightness forever,* for it desired to dwell there. And the King said: "I waited to see if it would come back to Israel, but it did not return. And again while I waited a light rose up in the heavens, and a sun emerged from the tribe of Judah, and it sent forth light which was very much brighter than before." And Israel, because of the brightness of that sun treated that sun with cruelty and would not walk in the light thereof. And that sun paid no heed to Israel, and the Israelites hated Him, and it became impossible that peace should exist between them and the sun.

They lifted up their hands against Him with staves and knives, and they wished to extinguish that sun. And they cast gloom upon the whole world with earthquake and thick darkness, and they imagined that that sun would never more rise upon them. And they destroyed His light and cast themselves upon Him and they set guard over His tomb wherein they had cast Him. He came forth where they did not look for him, and brightened the whole world, especially the First Sea and the Last Sea, Ethiopia and Rome: And He paid no heed whatsoever to Israel, and He ascended His former throne.

When Solomon the King saw this vision in his sleep his soul became disturbed, but his understanding was snatched away by a flash of lightning, and he woke up with an agitated mind. Moreover Solomon marvelled concerning the Queen, for she was vigorous in strength and beautiful of form, and she was undefiled in her virginity. She had reigned in her country for six years and, notwithstanding her gracious attraction and her splendid form, had kept her body pure. Then the Queen said unto Solomon: "Dismiss me, and let me depart to my country." And he went into his house and gave unto her whatsoever she wished for of splendid things and riches, beautiful apparel which bewitched the eyes and everything of great value; camels and wagons six thousand in number, which were laden with beautiful things of the most desirable kind, and wagons wherein loads were carried over the desert, and a vessel to travel over the sea.

29. SOLOMON'S SIGN TO THE QUEEN OF ETHIOPIA

The Queen rejoiced and she went forth in order to depart, and the King set her on her way with great pomp and ceremony. And Solomon took her aside so that they might be alone together, and he took off the ring that was upon his little finger and gave it to the Queen, and said unto her: " Take this ring so that thou mayest not forget me; and if it happens that I obtain seed from thee, this ring shall be unto it a sign; and if it shall be a man-child he shall come to me, and the peace of God be with thee! Whilst I was sleeping with thee I saw many visions in a dream, and it seemed as if a sun had risen upon Israel, but it snatched itself away and flew off and lighted up the country of Ethiopia; maybe that country shall be blessed through thee; God knoweth. As for thee, observe what I have told thee, so that thou mayest worship God with all thy heart and perform his will. For He punisheth those who are arrogant and He showeth compassion upon those who are humble, and He removeth the thrones of the mighty, and He maketh to be honoured those who are needy. For death and life are from Him, and riches and poverty are bestowed by His will. For everything is His and none can oppose His command and His judgment in the heavens, in the earth, in the sea or in the abysses; and may God be with thee! Go in Peace." Then they separated from each other.

30. THE QUEEN BRINGS FORTH HER SON
BAYNA-LEHKEM

And the Queen departed and came into the country of Bala Zadisareya nine months and five days after she had separated from King Solomon. And the pains of childbirth laid hold upon her, and she brought forth a man-child, and she gave it to the nurse with great pride and delight. There she tarried until the days of her purification were ended, then she came to her own country with great pomp and ceremony. And her officers who had remained there brought gifts to their Queen, and made obeisance to her, and paid homage to her, and all the regions of the country rejoiced at her coming. Those who were nobles among them, she arrayed in splendid apparel, and to some she gave gold and silver, and hyacinthine and purple robes; and she gave them all manner of things that could be desired. She ordered her kingdom right and none disobeyed her command, for she loved wisdom and God strengthened her kingdom.

And the child grew and she called his name Bayna-Lehkem, which means "son of the wise man." When the child reached the age of twelve years he went to the Queen his mother and said unto her: "O Queen, make me to know who is my father." And the Queen spoke to him angrily, wishing to frighten him so that he might not desire to go to his father saying: "Why dost thou ask me about thy father? I am thy father and thy mother; seek not to know any more." And the boy went forth from her presence, and sat down. A second time and a third time he asked her, and he implored her to tell him. One day however she told him, saying: "His country is far away, and the road is very difficult; wouldst thou not rather be here?" The youth Bayna-Lehkem was handsome; his whole body and his members, and the bearing of his shoulders resembled those of King Solomon, his father; and his eyes, his legs, and his whole posture resembled those of Solomon the King.

When he was twenty-two years old he was skilled in the art of war and horsemanship, in the hunting and trapping of wild beasts, and in everything that young men desire to learn. And he said unto the Queen: "I will go and look upon the face of my father, and I will come back here by the will of God, the Lord of Israel."

31. BAYNA-LEHKEM SETS OUT FOR JERUSALEM

And the Queen called Tamrin, the chief of her caravan and merchants and she said unto him: "Get ready for thy journey and take this young man with thee, for he bothers me by day and by night. And thou shalt take him to the King and shalt bring him back in safety, if the Lord God of Israel pleaseth." And she prepared a retinue suitable to their wealth and honourable condition, and made ready all the goods that were necessary for the journey and for presenting as gifts to the King. She made ready everything for sending him away, and she gave to the officers that were to accompany him enough money as they would need for him and for themselves on the journey. And she commanded them that they were not to leave him there, but only to take him to the King and then to bring him back again to her, when he would assume rulership over the land.

At that time there was a law in the country of Ethiopia that only a woman should reign, and that she must be a virgin who has never known man, but the Queen had said unto Solomon: "Henceforward a man who is of thy seed shall reign, and a woman shall nevermore reign in Ethiopia; only seed of thine shall reign and his seed after him from generation to generation. All this thou shalt inscribe in the scrolls and in the Book of their Prophets in brass, and thou shalt lay it in the House of God, which shall be built as a memorial and as a prophecy for the last days. And the people shall not worship the sun and the magnificence of the heavens, or the mountains and the forests, the stones and the trees of the wilderness, graven images and figures of gold, or the feathered fowl which fly; and they shall not make use of them in divining, and they shall not pay adoration unto them. And this law shall abide forever. And if there be anyone who shall transgress this law, thy seed shall judge him forever. Only give us the fringes of the covering of the holy heavenly Zion, the Tabernacle of the Law of God, which we would embrace. Peace be to the strength of thy kingdom and to thy brilliant wisdom, which God, the Lord of Israel, our Creator, hath given unto thee."

And the Queen took the young man aside and when he was alone with her she gave him that symbol which Solomon had given her, that is, the ring on his finger, so that he might know his son, and might remember her word and her covenant which she had made with him, that she would worship God all the days of her life, she and those who were under her dominion, with all the power which God had given her. And the Queen sent him away in peace.

The young man and his retinue made their way and they journeyed on and came into the country of the neighbourhood of Gaza. This is the Gaza which Solomon the King gave to the Queen of Ethiopia.

In the Acts of the Apostles, Luke the Evangelist wrote, saying: "He was the governor of the whole country of Gaza, an eunuch of Queen Candace who had believed on the word of Luke the Apostle.[1]

---

[1]Acts 8:26-39

32. BAYNA-LEHKEM ARRIVES IN GAZA

When the young man arrived in his mother's province of Gaza, he rejoiced there in the honour which he received, and in the gifts that were made to him. And when the people saw him they thought him to be the perfect likeness of Solomon the King. They made obeisance to him, and they said unto him: "Hail, the royal father liveth!" And they brought unto him gifts and offerings, fatted cattle and food, as they did to their king. And the people of the whole country of Gaza, as far as the border of Judah, were stirred up and said: "This is King Solomon." Then there were some who said: "The King is in Jerusalem building his house," and others said: "This is Solomon the King, the son of David." And they were perplexed, and they disputed with one another, and they sent off spies mounted on horses who were to seek out King Solomon and to find out if he were actually in Jerusalem, or if he were with them in Gaza.

When the spies came to the watchmen of the city of Jerusalem, they found King Solomon there and they made obeisance to him, and they said unto him: "Hail, may the royal father live! Our country is disturbed because there hath come into it a merchant who resembleth thee in form and appearance, without the slightest alteration or variation. He resembleth thee in noble carriage and in splendid form, and in stature and goodly appearance; he lacketh nothing in respect of thee and is in no way different from thyself. His eyes are bright like unto those of a man who hath drunk wine, his legs are graceful and slender, and the tower of his neck is like unto the tower of David thy father. He is like unto thee exactly in every respect, and every member of his whole body is like unto thine."

And Solomon the King answered and said unto them: "Where is it that he wisheth to go?" And they answered and said unto him: "We have not enquired of him, for he is awesome like thyself. But his own people, when we asked them, said: 'We have come from the dominions of Queen Candace of Ethiopia, and we are going to the country of Judah to King Solomon'." And when King Solomon heard this his heart was perturbed and he was glad in his soul, for in those days he had no children, except a boy who was seven years old and whose name was Rehoboam.

It happened to Solomon even as Paul said: "God hath made foolishness the wisdom of this world"[1] for Solomon had made a plan in his wisdom and said: "By one thousand women I shall father one thousand men-children, and I shall inherit the countries of the enemy, and I will over-throw their idols." But God only gave him three children. His eldest son was the King of Ethiopia, the son of the Queen of Ethiopia, and was the firstborn of whom God spake prophetically: "God sware unto David in righteousness, and repented not, ' Of the fruit of thy body will I make to sit upon thy throne'."[2] And God gave unto David His servant grace before Him, and granted unto him that there should sit upon the throne of Godhead one of his seed in the flesh, from the virgin, and He should judge the living and the dead, and reward every man according to his work, One to whom praise is meet, our Lord Jesus Christ for ever and ever. [3] *And He gave him one on the earth who should become king over the Tabernacle of the Law of the holy, heavenly Zion, that is to say, the King of Ethiopia.*

As for those who reigned and who were not of Israel, that happened because of the transgression of the law and the commandment, for which God was not pleased.

33. SOLOMON MAKES BAYNA-LEHKEM CAPTAIN OF HIS HOST

And Solomon the King sent the commander of his army with gifts and meat and drink to entertain the traveller. Then the commander set out with a great number of wagons and he came to Bayna-Lehkem, and embraced him, and gave him everything that Solomon the King had sent unto him. And he said unto him: "Make haste and come with me, for the heart of the King is burning up as with fire with the love of thee. Maybe he will find out for himself whether thou art his son or his brother; for in thy appearance and in thy conversation thou art in no way different from him.

And now, rise up quickly for my lord the King said unto me: 'Haste and bring him to me in honour and comfort and with suitable service, and in

---

[1] I Corinthians 1:20   [2] II Samuel 7:12-17   [3] Psalm 132:11

37

joy and gladness'." And the young man answered and said unto him: "I thank God, the Lord of Israel, that I have found grace with my lord the King without having seen his face; his word hath rejoiced me. And now I will put my trust in the Lord of Israel that he will show me the King, and will bring me back safely to my mother the Queen, and to my country Ethiopia."

And Benaiah, the son of Jehoiada,[1] Commander of the army of King Solomon, answered and said unto Bayna-Lehkem: "My Lord, this is a very small matter, and thou wilt find far greater joy and pleasure with my lord the King. And as concerning what thou sayest 'my country', Solomon the King is better than thy mother, and this our country is better than thy country. We have heard that thy country is a land of cold and cloud, of glare and burning heat, and a region of snow and ice. And when the sons of Noah, Shem, Ham and Japhet divided the world among them, they looked on thy country with wisdom and saw that although it was spacious and broad, it was a land of whirlwind and burning heat and therefore gave it to Canaan the son of Ham, as a portion for himself and his seed for ever. But the land that is ours is the land of inheritance, the promised land, which God hath given unto us according to the oath that He swore to our fathers, a land flowing with milk and honey, where food is ours without anxiety, a land that yieldeth fruit of every kind in its season without exhausting labour, a land which God keepeth watch over continually from one year to the next.

All this is thine, and we are thine and will be thine heirs, and thou shalt dwell in our country, for thou art the seed of David, the Lord of my Lord, and unto thee belongeth this throne of Israel."

And the headmen of the merchant Tamrin answered and said unto Benaiah: "Our country is the better. The air of our country is good for it is without burning heat or fire, and the water of our country is good and sweet, and floweth in rivers; moreover the tops of our mountains run with water. And we do not as in thy country, dig very deep wells in search of water, and we do not die through the heat of the sun; but even at noonday we hunt wild animals, buffaloes, gazelles, birds and small animals. And in the winter God protects us from one year to the next,

---

[1] I Kings 2:35

38

and in the springtime the people eat what they have trodden with the foot as in the land of Egypt. As for our trees they produce good crops of fruit; and the wheat, the barley and all the cattle are good and wonderful. But there is one thing that ye have wherein ye are better than we are, namely wisdom, and because of it we have come unto you."

Then Benaiah, the Commander of the army of King Solomon, answered saying: " What is better than wisdom? For wisdom hath established the earth and made strong the heavens, and restrained the waves of the sea so that it might not cover the earth. However, rise up and let us go to my lord, for his heart is greatly moved by love for thee, and he hath sent me to bring thee to him with all the speed possible."

And the son of the Queen rose up and arrayed Benaiah and the fifty men who were with him in gorgeous raiment, and they rose up to go to Jerusalem to Solomon the King. When they came close to the place where the horses were exercised and trained, Benaiah went on in front and came to the place where Solomon was, and he told him that the son of the Queen was handsome in his appearance, and that his voice was pleasant, and that he resembled him in form, and that his whole bearing was exceedingly noble. Then the King said unto him: "Where is he? Did I not send thee forth to bring him as quickly as possible?" And Benaiah said unto him: "He is here, I will bring him quickly." And Benaiah went and said unto the young man: "Rise up O my master, and come;" and making Bayna-Lehkem to go quickly he brought him to the King's gate. And when all the soldiers saw him they made obeisance unto him, and they said: "Behold, King Solomon hath gone forth from his palace." But when the men who were inside came forth they marvelled, and they went back to their places, and again they saw the King upon his throne; and wondering they went forth again and looked at the young man, and they were incapable of speaking and of saying anything.

When Benaiah came in again to announce to the King the arrival of the young man, there was none standing before the King, but all Israel had marched outside to see the young man.

34. SOLOMON'S CONVERSATION WITH BAYNA-LEHKEM

Benaiah went out and brought Bayna-Lehkem inside, and when King Solomon saw him he rose up and moved forward to welcome him, and he loosed the band of his apparel from his shoulder, and he embraced and kissed him, and said unto him: "Behold, my father David hath renewed his youth and hath risen from the dead." And Solomon the King turned around to those who had announced the arrival of the young man, and he said unto them: "Ye said unto me, 'He resembleth thee', but this is not my stature, but the stature of David my father in the days of his early manhood, and he is handsomer than I am." And Solomon the King rose up and went into his chamber, and he arrayed his son in apparel made of cloth embroidered with gold, and a belt of gold, and he set a crown upon his head, and a ring upon his finger.

Having arrayed him in glorious apparel which bewitched the eyes, he seated him upon his throne that he might be equal in rank to himself. Then he said unto the nobles and officers of Israel: "O ye who treat me with derision among yourselves and say that I have no son; look ye, this is my son, the fruit that hath gone forth from my body, whom God, the Lord of Israel hath given me when I expected it not."

And his nobles answered and said unto him: "Blessed be the mother who hath brought forth this young man, and blessed be the day wherein thou hadst union with the mother of this young man. For there hath risen upon us from the root of Jesse a shining man who shall be king of the posterity of his seed. And concerning his father none shall ask questions for verily he is an Israelite of the seed of David, fashioned perfectly in the likeness of his father's form and appearance; we are his servants and he shall be our King. And they brought unto him gifts, each according to his greatness.

The young man then took the ring which his mother had given him, and he said unto his father: "Take this ring and remember the word which thou didst speak unto the Queen, and give unto us a portion of the covering of the Tabernacle of the law of God, so that we may worship it all our days, and all those who are subject unto us, and those who are in the kingdom of the Queen." And the King answered and said unto him:

"Why givest thou me the ring as a sign? Without thy giving me a sign I discovered the likeness of thy form to myself, for thou art indeed my son."

Then the merchant Tamrin spake unto King Solomon saying: "Hearken O King, unto the message which thy handmaiden, the Queen my mistress sent by me: 'Take this young man, anoint him, consecrate and bless him, and make him King over our country, and give him the command that a woman shall never again reign in Ethiopia, and send him back in peace. And peace be with the might of thy kingdom, and with thy brilliant wisdom. As for me, I never wished that he should come where thou art, but he urged me exceedingly that he should be allowed to come to thee. Besides, I was afraid for him lest he should fall sick on the journey, either through thirst for water, or the heat of the sun, and I should bring my grey hairs down to the grave with sorrow. Then I put my trust in the holy, heavenly Zion, the Tabernacle of the Law of God, that thou wilt not withhold it in thy wisdom. For thy nobles do not return to their houses and look upon their children, by reason of the abundance of wisdom and food which thou givest them according to their desire. Because of this I, through my fear, sought assurance that thou mightest send him back to me in peace without sickness and suffering, in love and in peace that my heart might rejoice at having encountered thee'."

The King answered and said unto him: "Besides travailing with him and suckling him, what else hath a woman to do with a son? A daughter belongeth to the mother, and a boy to the father. God cursed Eve, saying: 'Bring forth children in anguish[1] and with sorrow of heart, and after thy bringing forth, shall take place thy return to thy husband. ' As for this son of mine, I will not give him to the Queen, but I will make him king over Israel. For this is my firstborn, the first of my race whom God hath given me."

Solomon sent unto the young man evening and morning dainty meats and apparel of honour, and gold and silver. And he said unto him: "It is better for thee to dwell here in our country with us, where the House of God is, and where God dwelleth."

---

[1]Genesis 3:16

Then the young man, his son, sent a message unto him, saying: "Gold and silver and rich apparel are not wanting in our country. But I came hither in order to hear thy wisdom, to see thy face, to salute thee and to pay homage to thy kingdom, and to make obeisance to thee, and then I intended thee to send me away to my mother and to my own country. For no man hateth the place where he was born, and everyone loveth the things of his native country. And though thou givest me dainty meats I do not love them, and they are not suitable for my body, but the meats whereby I grow and become strong are those that are gratifying to me. And although thy country pleaseth me even as a garden, yet my heart is not gratified; the mountains of the land of my mother where I was born are far better in my sight. As for the Tabernacle of the God of Israel, if I adore it where I am, it will give me glory, and I shall look upon the House of God which thou hast built, and I will make offering and supplication to it there.

As for Zion, the Tabernacle of the Law of God, give me a portion of the covering thereof, and I will worship it with my mother and with all those who are subject to my sovereignty. For my Lady the Queen hath already rooted out all those who served idols, and those who worshipped strange objects. For she had heard from thee and had learned, and she did according to thy word, and we worship the living God." And the King was not able to make his son consent to remain in Jerusalem.

35. SOLOMON QUESTIONS HIS SON BAYNA-LEHKEM

Again Solomon held converse with his son when he was alone, and he said unto him: "Why dost thou wish to depart from me? What dost thou lack here that thou wouldst go back to the country of the heathen? What is it that driveth thee to forsake the Kingdom of Israel?" And his son answered and said unto him: "It is impossible for me to live here. I must go back to my mother, thou favouring me with thy blessing. For thou hast a son who is better than I am, namely Rehoboam who was born of thy wife lawfully, whilst my mother is not thy wife according to the law."

And the King answered and said unto him: " Since thou speakest in this manner, according to the law I myself am not the son of my father

David, for he took the wife of another man whom he caused to be slain in battle, and he begot me by her;[1] but God is compassionate and He hath forgiven him. Who is wickeder and more foolish than men? And who is as compassionate and wise as God? God hath made me of my father, and thee hath He made of me, according to His will. O my son, thou fearer of our Lord God, do not violence to the face of thy father, so that in times to come thou mayest not meet with violence from him that shall go forth from thy loins, and that thy seed may prosper upon the earth. My son Rehoboam is a boy six years old, and *thou art my first-born son. Thou hast come to reign and to lift up the spear of him that begot thee. Behold, I have been reigning for twenty-nine years, and thy mother came to me in the seventh year of my kingdom;* and please God, He shall make me to attain to the span of the days of my father. And when I shall be gathered to my fathers, thou shalt sit upon my throne, and thou shalt reign in my stead, and the elders of Israel shall love thee exceedingly; and I will make a marriage for thee, and will give thee as many queens and concubines as thou desirest. And thou shalt be blessed in this land of inheritance with the blessing that God gave unto our fathers, even as He covenanted with Noah His servant, and with Abraham His friend, and with the righteous men and their descendants after them, down to David my father. Thou seest me, a weak man, upon the throne of my fathers, and thou shalt be like myself after me, and thou shalt judge nations without number, and families that cannot be counted.

And the Tabernacle of the God of Israel shall belong to thee and thy seed forever. And God shall dwell within it and shall hear thy prayers therein, and thy memorial shall be in it from generation to generation."

And his son answered and said unto him: "O Lord, it is impossible for me to leave my country and my mother, for my mother made me to swear by her breasts that I would not remain here but would return to her quickly, and also that I would not marry a wife here. And the Tabernacle of the God of Israel shall bless me wheresoever I shall be, and thy prayer shall accompany me always. I desired to see thy face, to hear thy voice and to receive thy blessings; and now I desire to depart to my mother in safety."

---

[1]II Samuels 11:1-27

43

36. SOLOMON SENDS NOBLES OF ISRAEL TO ETHIOPIA WITH HIS SON

Solomon the King went back into his palace, and he gathered together his councillors, his officers and the elders of his kingdom, and he said unto them: "I am not able to make my son consent to dwell here. And now, hearken ye unto me and to what I shall say unto you. Let us make him king of the country of Ethiopia, together with your children; ye sit on my right hand and on my left hand, and in like manner the eldest of your children shall sit on his right hand and on his left hand. Ye councillors and officers, let us give him your firstborn children and we shall have two kingdoms; I will rule here with you, and our children shall rule there. And I put my trust in God that a third time He will give me seed, and that a third king will be to me.

Baltasor the king of Rome wisheth that I would give my son to his daughter, and to make him with his daughter king over the whole country of Rome. For besides her he hath no other child, and he hath sworn that he will only make king a man who is of the seed of David my father. And if we rule there we shall be three kingdoms. And Rehoboam shall reign here over Israel. For thus saith the prophecy of David my father: 'The seed of Solomon shall become three heads of kingdoms upon the earth.' And we will send unto them priests, and we will ordain laws for them, and they shall worship and serve the God of Israel under three royal heads.

And God shall be praised by the race of his people Israel, and be exalted in all the earth, even as my father wrote in his book, saying: 'Tell the nations that God is King.[1] Announce to the peoples His work, praise Him and sing ye unto Him;' and again he saith: 'Praise God with a new song. His praise is in the congregation of the righteous, Israel shall rejoice in his Creator.'[2] Unto us belongeth the glory of sovereignty and we will praise our Creator. And the nations who serve idols shall look upon us and they shall fear us and make us kings over them, and they shall praise God and fear Him.

---

[1]Compare Psalm 95   [2]Compare Psalm 96

Now, come ye, let us make this young man king, and let us send him away with your children, ye who possess wealth and position. According to the position and wealth that ye have here, shall your children rule there. And they shall see the ordering of royalty, and we will establish them according to our law, and we will direct them and give them commands and send them away to reign there."

And the priests, the officers and the councillors answered and said unto him: "Do send thy firstborn, and we will send our children also according to thy wish, for who can resist the command of God and the King? They are the servants of thee and of thy seed as thou hast proclaimed. If thou wishest, thou canst sell them and their mothers to be slaves; it is not for us to transgress thy command and the command of the Lord thy God." *And then they prepared their children to send them into the country of Ethiopia, so that they might reign there and dwell there forever, they and their seed from generation to generation."* [1]

37. BAYNA-LEHKEM (MENYELEK I) IS ANOINTED KING OF ETHIOPIA AND IS CALLED DAVID II

And they made ready the ointment of the oil of kingship, and the sounds of the large horn and the small horn, the flute and the pipes, and the harp and the drums filled the air; and the city resounded with cries of joy and gladness. And they brought the young man into the Holy of Holies, and he laid hold upon the horns of the altar, and sovereignty was given unto him by the mouth of Zadok the high priest, and by the mouth of Benaiah the priest, the commander of the army of King Solomon, and he anointed him with the holy oil of kingship.

Then he went out from the house of the Lord, and they called his name David, for the name of a king came to him by the law. They made him to ride upon the mule of King Solomon and they led him round about the city, and said: "We have appointed thee from this moment;" and then they cried out to him: "Long live the royal father!" And there were some who said: "It is right that thy dominion of Ethiopia shall be from the river of Egypt to the setting sun, and from Shoa to the East of India,

---

[1]Falashas (Ethiopian Jews – see Appendix 2)

for thou wilt please the people of these lands. And the Lord God of
Israel and the Tabernacle of the Law of God shall be unto thee a guide,
and shall be with all that thou lookest upon. All thine enemies and foes
shall be overthrown before thee, and completion and perfection shall be
unto thee and unto thy seed after thee; thou shalt judge many nations
and none shall judge thee. The blessing of heaven and earth shall be thy
blessing." And all the congregation of Israel said: "Amen." Then his
father Solomon the King also said unto Zadok the priest: "Make him to
know and tell him concerning the judgment and decree of God which he
shall observe in Ethiopia."

38. ZADOK'S COMMANDS TO DAVID II

Zadok the priest said unto the young man: "Hearken unto what I shall
say unto thee; and if thou wilt perform it thou shalt live to God, and if
thou dost not, God will punish thee and thou shalt be vanquished by thy
foes. And God shall turn away His face from thee, and thou shalt be
dismayed, sad and sorrowful in thy heart, and thy sleep shall be without
rest. So then, hearken unto the word of God and perform that which we
command thee this day and serve no other gods. But if thou will not hear
the word of God, then hearken to all the curses here mentioned which
shall come upon thee: cursed shalt thou be in the field and in the city.
Cursed shall be the fruit of thy land and the fruit of thy belly, the herds of
thy cattle and the flocks of thy sheep. And God shall send upon thee
famine and pestilence, and He shall destroy that whereto thou hast put
thy hand, until at length He shall destroy thee, because thou hast not
hearkened to His word. And the heavens which are above thee shall
become brass, and the earth which is beneath thee shall become iron;
and God shall make the rain which should fall upon thy land to be
darkness only, and dust shall descend from heaven upon thee until it
shall cover thee up and destroy thee. And thou shalt be smitten in battle
before thine enemies. Thou shalt go forth to attack them by one road,
and by seven roads shalt thou take to flight before their faces, and thou
shalt be routed; thy dead body shall become food for the fowls of the
heavens, and there shall be none to bury thee. And God shall punish
thee with sores (leprosy), with the wasting disease, with the fever that
destroyeth, and with the punishments, the plagues of Egypt. With

46

blindness and terror of heart thou shalt grope about by day like a blind man in the darkness, and thou shalt find none to help thee in thy trouble.

Thou shalt marry a wife, and another man shall carry her away by force. Thou shalt build a house and shalt not dwell therein. Thou shalt plant a vineyard and shalt not harvest the grapes thereof. Men shall slay thy fat oxen before thine eyes, and thou shalt not eat of their flesh. Men shall snatch away thy ass and shall not bring him back to thee. Thy sheep shall run to the slaves and to thine enemy, and thou shalt find none to help thee, and thy sons and daughters shall follow other people, and thou shalt see with thine own eyes how they are smitten, and shalt be able to do nothing. An enemy whom thou knowest not shall devour the food of thy land and thy labour, and thou shalt not be able to prevent him; and thou shalt become a man of suffering and calamity.

All these things shall come upon thee if thou wilt not hearken to the word of the Lord. But if thou wilt truly hearken unto the word of the Lord, the goodness of God shall find thee, and thou shalt rule the countries of the enemy, and thou shalt inherit glory everlasting from the Lord God of Israel, Who ruleth everything for He is the Lord of death and of life, and He directeth and ruleth all the world with His wisdom, His power and His mighty arm."

39. THE BLESSING OF KINGS

"Hearken thou now to the blessing that shall come upon thee, if thou wilt do the Will of God... Thou shalt be blessed in all thy ways; blessed shalt thou be in the city and in the field and in thy house, and blessed shall be the fruit of thy land, the fountains of thy waters and the fruit that thou hast planted. Blessed shall be the flocks of thy sheep, thy granaries and thy barns. Blessed shalt thou be in thy coming and in thy going forth.

And God shall bring to thee thine enemies who have risen up against thee, and they shall be trodden small beneath thy feet. God shall send His blessing on thy houses and on everything to which thou hast put thy hand, and He shall multiply for thee good things, namely, children of thy body, produce of thy land, and births among thy flocks and herds. And in the land which He swore to give to thy fathers, God shall open for thee the storehouse of the blessings of the heavens, and He shall give thee blessed rain, and shall bless the fruit of thy labour. Thou shalt lend unto many people, but thou shalt not borrow. Thou shalt rule over many nations, but they shall not rule over thee.

And God shall set thee at the head and not at the tail, and thou shalt be at the top and not at the bottom. And thou shalt gather together of every blessing of the land for thy flocks and herds, and thou shalt take the spoil of the nations for thy army, and they shall bow down to thee and to thy sovereignty because of the greatness of thy glory. *Thine honour shall rise up like the cedar and like the morning star;[1] the brilliance of thy glory shall be before all the nations of the earth, and before every tribe of thy people Israel.*

For God shall be with thee in all thy ways, and He shall perform thy will in everything that thou desirest. And thou shalt inherit the countries of thine enemy, and the magnificence of thy people shall be praised because of the greatness of thine awesomeness, and because of the multitude of thy soldiers. And all those who do not perform the Will of God, will fear thee because thou dost do His Will, and dost serve Him, and therefore He will give thee great majesty in the sight of those who see thee. Their hearts shall tremble before the bridle of thy horses and the quiver of thy bow. At the glitter of thy shield they shall bow down to the face of the earth, for their hearts shall be terrified at the sight of thy dreadful majesty.

When those who are in the mountains see thee afar off they shall come down to the plain, and those who are on the seas and in the deep waters shall come forth, so that the Lord may bring them into thy hand because they have transgressed the command of God. And thou, when thou doest His Will, shall receive from Him everything that thou hast asked; for if thou lovest Him He will love thee, and if thou keepest His commandments He will grant thee the petition of thy heart, and everything that thou seekest thou shalt receive from Him.

---

[1]Revelation 2:26-28; 22:16

40. THE TEN COMMANDMENTS

Hear ye Israel, that which God commanded you to keep; He saith: 'I am the Lord thy God Who hast brought thee out of the land of Egypt and out of the House of Bondage. There shall be no other gods besides me, and thou shalt not make any god that is graven, and no god that is like what is in the heavens above, or in the earth beneath, or in the water that is under the earth. Thou shalt not bow down to them, and thou shalt not serve them, for I the Lord thy God am a jealous God. I am He who visits the sins of the fathers upon the children to the third and fourth generation of those who hate Me, and I perform mercy to a thousand generations of those who love Me, and keep My commandments.'

'Thou shalt not swear a false oath in the name of the Lord thy God, for the Lord will not hold innocent the man who sweareth a false oath in His Name.'

'Observe the day of the Sabbath to sanctify it, even as the Lord thy God commanded. Six days thou shalt do thy work, and on the seventh day, the Sabbath of the Lord thy God, thou shalt do no work at all, neither thyself, nor thy son, nor thy daughter, nor thy servant, nor thy ass, nor thy beast, nor the stranger that abideth with thee. For in six days God made the heavens and the earth, and the sea and all that is in them, and rested on the seventh day, and because of this God blessed the seventh day and declared it free from work.'

'Honour thy father and thy mother so that it may be good unto thee, the many days that thou shalt find in the land which the Lord thy God hath given thee.'

'Thou shalt not go with the wife of another man.'

'Thou shalt not slay a life.'

'Thou shalt not commit fornication.'

'Thou shalt not steal.'

'Thou shalt not bear false witness against thy neighbour.'

'Thou shalt not covet thy neighbour's wife, nor his house, nor his land, his manservant nor his maidservant his ox nor his cattle, nor his ass, nor any of the beasts that thy neighbour has acquired.'[1]

This is the word which God hath spoken, His law and regulations. And those who sin He rebuketh, so that they may not be confirmed in error, and may restrain themselves from the pollution wherewith God is not pleased. And this is the thing with which God is not pleased, and it is right that men should abstain from it.

'No man shall uncover the shame of one with whom he hath kinship; for I am the Lord thy God. The shame of thy father and thy mother thou shalt not uncover, for it is thy mother. Thou shalt not uncover the shame of thy father's wife, for it is the shame of thy mother. Thou shalt not uncover the shame of thy sister who was begotten by thy father or thy mother. Whether she was born unto him from outside or whether she is a kinswoman of thine, thou shalt not uncover her shame.

Thou shalt not uncover the shame, neither of thy son's daughter or the shame of the daughter and the wife of thy brother's son, for it is thine own shame.

Thou shalt not uncover the shame of thy brother's wife, for it is thy brother's shame as long as thy brother liveth. Thou shalt not uncover the shame of a woman and that of her daughter; thou shalt not cause their shame to be uncovered; it is thy house and it is sin.

Thou shalt not take to wife a maiden and her sister so as to make them jealous each of the other, and thou shalt not uncover their shame, nor the shame of the one or the other as long as the first sister is alive. Thou shalt not go to a menstruous woman, until she is purified; thou shalt not uncover her shame whilst she is still unclean. And thou shalt not go to the wife of thy neighbour to lie with her, and thou shalt not let thy seed enter her.

Thou shalt not lie with a man as with a woman, for it is pollution, and thou shalt not go to a beast nor lie with it so as to make thy seed go out

---

[1]Exodus 20:2-17

50

upon it, that thou mayest not be polluted thereby. And a woman shall not go to a beast to lie with it, for it is pollution. And ye shall not pollute yourselves with any of these things, for with them the nations whom I have driven out before you, have polluted themselves, and with them ye shall not pollute your bodies.'

And sanctify ye your souls and your bodies to God for He is the Holy One, and He loveth those who sanctify their souls and their bodies to Him. For He is holy and to be feared, He is high, merciful and compassionate, and to Him praise is due for ever and ever. Amen."

PART III

African Zion

"Ethiopia shall soon stretch out her hands
unto God."

Psalm 68:31

41. THE PRIESTS AND OFFICIALS OF THE COURT OF DAVID II IN ETHIOPIA

And the city rejoiced because the King had made his son King, and had appointed him King from his own territory to that of another. But the city sorrowed also because the King had commanded that they should give their children who were called "firstborn." And those who were on the right hand should sit in the same way as their fathers sat with King Solomon, even so should they sit at the right hand of his son David II, the King of Ethiopia; and those who were on the left hand should sit as their father sat with King Solomon, even so should they sit at the left hand of his son David II, the King of Ethiopia; and their rank and names should be like those of their fathers. And each should be according to his ordinance, his greatness, his possession of authority; in this wise shall they be. As Solomon did to his nobles, so shall David do to his nobles, and as Solomon ordained for his governors, so shall David order the direction of his kingdom.

These are the names of those who were appointed to be sent away to Ethiopia:

Azariah, the son of *Zadok* the priest, who was the High Priest;
Elyas, the son of *Arni* the Archdeacon (the father of *Arni* was the archdeacon of *Nathan* the Prophet);
Adram, the son of *Arderones*, leader of the people;
Fankera, the son of *Soba*, scribe of the oxen;
Akonhel, the son of *Tofel*, the youth;
Samneyas, the son of *Akitalam*, the recorder;
Fikaros, the son of *Neya*, commander of the armed men, chief of the troops;
Lewandos, the son of *Akire*, commander of the recruits;
Fakuten, the son of *Adray*, commander of the sea;
Matan, the son of *Benyas*, chief of the house;
Adaraz, the son of *Kirem*, master of decorations;
Dalakem, the son of *Matrem*, chief of the horse-soldiers;
Adaryos, the son of *Nedros*, chief of the foot-soldiers;
Awsteran, the son of *Yodad*, bearer of "the Glory";
Astarayon, the son of *Asa*, messenger of the palace;

Imi, the son of *Matatyas*, commander of the host;
Makri, the son of *Abisa*, judge of the palace;
Abis, the son of *Karyos*, assessor of tithes and taxes;
Lik Wendeyos, the son of *Nelenteyos*, judge of assembly;
Karmi, the son of *Hadneyas*, chief of the royal workmen;
Seranyas, the son of *Akazel*, administrator of the King's house.

These are all those who were given to David II (Menyelek I), King of Ethiopia, the son of Solomon, King of Israel. And Solomon also gave him horses, chariots, riding camels, mules, wagons for carrying loads, gold, silver and splendid apparel, byssus,[1] purple, gems, pearls and precious stones; and he gave his son everything that would be wished for in the country of Ethiopia.

Then they made ready to set out, and though there was great joy with the nobles of the King of Ethiopia, there was sadness with the nobles of the King of Israel, because through the firstborn son of Solomon, King of Israel, that is to say, the King of Ethiopia, the firstborn sons of the nobles of Israel were given to rule over the country of Ethiopia with the son of Solomon the King. Then they assembled together and wept, together with their fathers and their mothers, their kinsfolk and their peoples and their countrymen.

And they cursed the King secretly and reviled him because he had seized their sons against their will. But unto the King they said: "Because of this thou hast done well. Thy wisdom is so good that the Kingdom of Israel, by the Will of God and by thy wisdom, extendeth to the country of Ethiopia. And God will gather the other kingdoms of the world into thy hand for thou hast a right mind towards God, and thou wishest that they shall serve the God of Israel, and that idols may be destroyed out of the world."

And they praised him and said unto him: "Now know we that God spoke concerning thee to our father Abraham when He said: 'In thy seed shall all the nations of the earth be blessed'."[2] And they made their

---

[1] A valuable and fine fabric, like linen, made by the ancients.
[2] Genesis 12:1

faces to appear happy, and they jested before him, and they praised him exceedingly because of his wisdom. But when they said these things unto him, he understood them in his wisdom, and bore with them patiently, as God beareth with us patiently knowing well all our sins.

And the whole earth, the heavens and the ends of the world, the sea and the dry land are the kingdom of God. He judgeth. And He hath given the earth to the King to be subject unto him, that he may judge those who do evil, and those who do good he may reward them with good. For the Spirit of God resteth in the heart of the king, and His hands are in his mind, and His knowledge is in his understanding.

42. THE KING MUST NOT BE REVILED

It is not a good thing to revile the king, for he is the anointed of God. It is neither seemly nor good. If he doeth that which is good he will not suffer loss in three kingdoms; first, God shall overthrow for him his enemy. Secondly, God shall make him reign with Him and with His righteousness, and shall make him to sit on His right hand. Thirdly, God shall make him to reign upon earth with glory and joy, and shall direct his kingdom for him, and shall bring down the nations under his feet. But if he treateth God lightly, and doth not do that which is good, and doth not himself walk in the path of uprightness, God shall work as He pleaseth against him; on earth He will make his days to be few, and in eternity his place of abode shall be the habitation of Sheol with the Devil; and on earth he shall enjoy neither health nor gladness and he shall live in fear and terror, without peace and with perturbation.

It is not a good thing for any of those who are under the dominion of a king to revile him, for retribution belongeth to God. But the priests are like the prophets, for mysteries are given unto them, so that they may hold upon the Sun of righteousness, whilst the Seraphim, who were created out of fire, are only able to lay hold upon the mysteries with fire-tongs. As for the priests He named them "salt," "lamp" and also "light of the world," and "the sun that lighteneth the darkness;" Christ the Sun of righteousness being in their hearts. And a priest who hath in him understanding rebuketh the king concerning the work that he hath seen;

and that which he hath not seen God will enquire into, and there is none who can call Him to account. Moreover, the people must not revile the priests for they are the children of God and the men of His house, for which reason they must rebuke men for their sins and errors.

And thou, O priest, if thou seest sin in a well-known man, do not hesitate to rebuke him; let neither sword nor exile make thee afraid. And hear how angry God was with Isaiah because he did not rebuke King Uzziah. And hearken also concerning Samuel the prophet, how he rebuked Saul[1] the king, being in no way afraid of him, and how he rent his kingdom from him by his word; and hearken also how Elijah rebuked Ahab.[2]

So, fear not, and rebuke and teach him that transgresseth. And Israel from of old reviled their kings and provoked their prophets to wrath, and in later times they crucified their Saviour.

43. THE CONSPIRACY OF THE SONS OF THE NOBLES WHO ARE TO GO TO ETHIOPIA

And the children of the nobles of Israel, who were commanded to depart with the son of the king, took counsel together, saying: "What shall we do? For we must leave our country and our birthplace, and our family and the people of our city. Let us sorrow on account of our Lady Zion, because they are making us to leave her. For in her they have committed us to God, and we have served her to this day. It is because of her and our departure that they have specially made us to weep." And the others answered and said unto them: "Verily she is our Lady and our hope, and our object of boasting, and we have grown up under her blessings. And how is it possible for us to forsake Zion our Mistress? For we have been given to her. And what shall we do? If we resist his command the King will kill us, and we are unable to transgress the word of our fathers or the King's command. And what shall we do concerning Zion?"

---

[1] I Samuel, Chapter 15   [2] I Kings, Chapter 17

Then Azariah, the son of Zadok the priest, answered and said: "I will counsel you what we shall do. But make a covenant with me to the end of your lives; and swear to me that ye will not repeat it whether we be taken captives or whether we go forth unhindered." And they swore an oath to him in the Name of the Lord God of Israel, and by the heavenly Zion, the Tabernacle of the Law of God, and by what God had promised unto Abraham, and by the purity and excellence of Isaac, and by His making Jacob to arrive in and inherit a land whereto he was a stranger, and his seed after him.

When they had sworn thus to him, he answered and said unto them: "Come now, let us take with us our Lady Zion. How are we to take her? I will show you. Carry ye out my plan and if God willeth we shall be able to take our Lady with us. And if they should gain knowledge of our doing and slay us, that shall not trouble us, because we shall die for our Lady Zion." And they all rose up, and they said unto him: "We will do everything that thou hast counseled us to do; whether we die or whether we live, we are with thee for the sake of our Lady Zion. If we die it will not cause us sorrow, and if we live the Will of God be done!" And one of them, the son of Benaiah, whose name was Zechariah, said: "I cannot sit down because of the great gladness that is in my heart.

Tell me, canst thou indeed carry her off and go into the House of God instead of thy father Zadok, with the keys in thy hand? Thou knowest the hidden window which King Solomon made, but none of the priests may enter therein except thy father once each year on the Day of Atonement, in order to offer up sacrifice in the Holy of Holies on behalf of himself and on behalf of the people. Ponder, consider, and sleep not in the matter of thy wish to carry away Zion. And we will depart with her as soon as she hath been committed to our care, and we shall have joy and our fathers sorrow when she arrives with us in the country of Ethiopia."

Azariah then said unto them: "Do ye what I tell you, and we shall succeed. Give ye to me ten didrachmas,[1] and I will give them to a carpenter so that he will make haste to prepare for me good planks of

---

[1]Double drachmas; ancient Greek silver coins weighing two drachmas.

59

wood, because of his love of money he will fasten them together very quickly of the height, width, length and size of our Lady Zion. I will give him the dimensions myself, and I will say unto him: "Prepare for me pieces of wood for a framework so that I may make a raft for we are going to travel over the sea, and in the event of the ship sinking I shall be able to get up on the raft, and we shall be saved from the sea. I will take the framework without the pieces of wood being fixed together, and I will have them put together.

Then I will set them down in the habitation of Zion, and will drape them with the draperies of Zion, and I will take Zion, and will dig a hole in the ground and set Zion there, until we journey and take it away with us, but I will not tell the matter to the king until we have travelled far."

They each gave him ten didrachmas, and this money amounted to one hundred and forty didrachmas which he gave to a carpenter who fashioned a good piece of work from the remains of the wood of the house of the sanctuary, and Azariah rejoiced and showed it to his brethren.

44. THE PLOT TO REMOVE THE TABERNACLE OF ZION FROM THE TEMPLE IN JERUSALEM

While Azariah was asleep at night the Angel of the Lord appeared unto him, and said unto him: "Take four goats, each a yearling, they shall be for your sins; and four pure sheep, yearlings also, and an ox where on no yoke hath ever been laid. And thou shalt offer up the ox as a sacrifice on the east side of Zion, and the sheep and the goats to the right and left thereof, and to the west of it, which is close to its exit . And your Lord David (Menyelek) shall speak to Solomon the King and shall say unto him: 'One thing I ask from thee father, I would offer up a sacrifice to the holy city Jerusalem, and to my Lady Zion, the holy and heavenly Tabernacle of the Law of God.' And Solomon shall say unto him: 'Do so.' Then David shall say unto him: 'Let the son of the priest offer up sacrifice on my behalf, even as he knoweth'; and he will give thee the command, and thou shalt offer up the sacrifice.

And thou shalt bring forth the Tabernacle of the Law of God after thou hath offered up the sacrifice, *and I will again show thee what thou shalt do in respect of bringing it out; for this is from God. For Israel hath provoked God to wrath, and for this reason He will make the Tabernacle of the Law of God to depart from them."*

When Azariah awoke from his dream he rejoiced greatly and his heart and mind were clear. He remembered everything that the Angel of the Lord had shown him in the night, and how he had sealed him and given him strength and heartened him. So he went to his brethren and when they were gathered together he told them everything that the Angel of God had shown him; how the Tabernacle of the Law of God, and the kingdom of Solomon was to be seized by them, with the exception of two "rods," and how the kingdom of Israel was to be divided. Then Azariah said: "Rejoice with me. I rejoice because it has been shown to me thus; for the grace of their priesthood and kingdom shall depart with us, and it shall be by the will of God. Thus said the Angel unto me. Now, let us go and tell David our Lord so that he may say to his father, 'I will offer up a sacrifice'."

So they went and told David the son of Solomon and he rejoiced and he sent for Benaiah, that he might send him to his father, and he came. And David sent him to his father Solomon, and he said unto the king: "There is one petition which I would make unto thee, for I thy servant am going to depart, and wish to offer up a sacrifice of propitiation for my sins in this thy holy city of Jerusalem and of Zion, the Tabernacle of the Law of God. And peace be with thy majesty."

45. THE OFFERING OF AZARIAH AND THE KING

And Benaiah went and told King Solomon, and the King rejoiced over it and commanded them to make ready the altar of sacrifice so that his son might make his offering. And he brought and gave unto him that which he had vowed to God; one hundred bulls, one hundred oxen, ten thousand sheep, ten thousand goats, ten of every kind of animal that may be eaten and ten of every kind of clean bird, so that he might offer libations and sacrifices to the God of Israel; and twenty silver jugs of fine white flour, each weighing twenty shekels, and forty baskets of bread.

All these things did Solomon the King give unto his son David. Again David sent a message saying: "Let Azariah the priest offer up sacrifice on my behalf;" and Solomon said unto him: "Do that which thou wishest." And Azariah rejoiced because of this and he went and brought from his father's flock an ox whereon no yoke had ever been laid, and four yearlings of the goats and four clean yearlings of the sheep.

And the King went to offer up sacrifice, and the priests made themselves ready and the people were gathered together, and the birds of the heavens rejoiced and they were all united in their great gladness that day.

Then Azariah mingled his offerings with the offerings of the King and he made an offering with his vessels, even as the Angel of God had commanded him to do. After they had offered up their sacrifices they went back to their houses and slept.

46. HOW THEY REMOVED THE TABERNACLE OF ZION

And behold, the Angel of the Lord appeared again to Azariah and he stood up above him like a pillar of fire, and he filled the house with his light . And he raised up Azariah and said unto him: "Stand up, be strong and rouse up Elmeyas and Abis and Makri, and take the pieces of wood and I will open for thee the doors of the sanctuary. And take thou the Tabernacle of the Law of God, and thou shalt carry it without trouble and discomfort. And as I have been commanded by God to be with it forever, I will be thy guide when thou shalt carry it away."

Azariah rose up quickly and woke up the three men, his brethren, and they took the pieces of wood and went into the house of God (they found all the doors open, both those that were outside and those that were inside), to the actual place where Azariah found Zion, the Tabernacle of the Law of God; and it was taken by them forthwith, in the twinkling of an eye, the Angel of the Lord being present and directing.

Had it not been that God willed it, Zion could not have been taken away. And the four of them carried Zion away and they brought it into the house of Azariah, then they went back into the house of God and they set up the frame of wood on the place where Zion had been, and covered it over with the covering of Zion, and they shut the doors and went back to their houses. After this they took lamps and set them in the place where Zion was hidden, and they sacrificed the sheep and burned offerings of incense, then they spread purple cloths over it and set it in a secret place for seven days and seven nights.

47. HOW SOLOMON BLESSED HIS SON DAVID II

And then the King of Ethiopia rose up to depart to his country and he came to his father that he might pray on his behalf, and he said unto him: "Bless me, father," and he made obeisance unto him. And the King raised him up, blessed him and embraced him, and said: "Blessed be the Lord my God Who blessed my father David, and Who blessed our father Abraham. May He be with thee always, and bless thy seed even as He blessed Jacob and made his seed to be as many as the stars of heaven and the sand of the sea. And as Abraham blessed Isaac my father, even so shall thy blessing be as the dew of heaven and the spaciousness of the earth, and may all animals and all birds of the heavens, the beasts of the field and the fish of the sea, be in subjection unto thee. Be thou full, perfect and gracious, pure, righteous and merciful; not oppressive, not perverse and not prone to wrath. And the enemy shall be afraid of thee and thy adversaries shall cast themselves under the sole of thy feet. And my Lady Zion, the holy and heavenly, the Tabernacle of the Law of God, shall be a guide unto thee at all times; a guide in respect of what thou should think in thy heart and should do with thy fingers." And David was blessed, and he made obeisance and departed.

48. THE FAREWELL OF DAVID II; THE GRIEF OF THE PEOPLE

The Ethiopians bade the King farewell and departed; but first of all they had set Zion by night upon a chariot along with other common merchandise and stores of every sort and kind. When all the wagons were loaded, the masters of the caravan rose up and the horn was blown and the city became excited; the youth shouted loudly and awesomeness and grace crowned and surrounded Zion. And the old men wailed, the children cried out, the widows wept and the virgins lamented because the sons of their nobles, the mighty men of Israel had risen up to depart. But the city did not weep for them alone, but because the majesty of the city had been carried off with them. And although they did not know yet that Zion had been taken from them, they felt sorrow in their hearts and they wept bitterly; and they were then as when God slew the firstborn of Egypt, for there was not a house wherein there was not wailing, from man even to the beast; the dogs howled and the asses brayed, and all those who were left there mingled their tears together.

It was as though the general of a mighty army had besieged the great city and had captured it by assault and looted it, and taken its people prisoners and slain them with the edge of the sword; even thus was that city of Zion, Jerusalem.

King Solomon was dismayed at the weeping and outcry of the city, and he looked out from the roof of the palace, the fort of the King's house, and saw the whole city weeping and following them. And as a child whom his mother has removed from her breast and left, followeth in her footsteps crying out and weeping, even so did the people cry out and weep, and they cast dust upon their heads and shed tears with their eyes.

When Solomon saw the majesty of those who had departed, he was deeply moved and he trembled and his bowels quaked while his tears fell drop by drop upon his apparel, and he said: "Woe is me! For my glory hath departed and the crown of my splendour hath fallen. My belly is burned up because this my son hath departed, and the majesty of my city and the nobles, the children of my might, are removed. *From this moment our glory hath passed away, and our kingdom hath been*

64

carried off unto a strange people who know not God, even as the prophet said, 'The people who had not sought Me have found Me.'[1] From this time forth the law and wisdom and understanding shall be given unto them. And my father prophesied concerning them, saying: 'Ethiopia shall bow before Him, and His enemies shall eat the dust.[1] And in another place he said: 'Ethiopia shall stretch out her hands to God, and He shall receive her with honour, and the kings of the earth shall praise God.'[2] And again he said: 'Behold the Philistines,[3] and the Tyrians, and the people of Ethiopia, who were born without the Law.

The Law shall be given unto them, and they shall call unto Zion, because of a man who shall be born.'[4] Will this man then be my son who is begotten of me?"

49. DAVID II (MENYELEK I) RECEIVES THE COVERING OF THE TABERNACLE OF ZION

Then King Solomon said unto Zadok the priest: "Go, bring the covering that is upon Zion, and take this covering which is better than that one, and lay it over the two cherubs which are below it." This covering was made of threads of the finest gold wirework twisted together and hammered out into a pattern. "And the five mice which were given to Zion, and the ten figures of their shame, the emerods which the nobles of the Philistines made for their redemption (on the fringes are figures of gold that came forth from the land of Kades, which Moses in Sinai commanded should be made in the fringe of the apparel of Aaron his brother); gather all these together in the covering of Zion and give them to my son David. For his mother said in her message by Tamrin her servant: 'Fetch us some of the fringe of the covering of Zion, so that we may worship it, we and those who are in subjection unto us and all our kingdom.' And now, give it to him and say unto him: 'Take this covering of Zion, for thy mother sent a message concerning this, and had said unto thee thyself: 'Give us some of the fringe of its covering, which we can worship, so that we may not like the heathen worship another God.'

---

[1]Psalm 72:9   [2]Psalm 68:31; 72:10   [3]Psalm 83:7   [4]Psalm 87:2-6

And Zion, the Tabernacle of the Law of God, shall be unto thee a guide wheresoever thou art. But it must remain with us perpetually although we have not paid it all the honour which is its due; and you, although it be not with you, must honour it and revere it according to what is due to it and what is true. For God said unto Eli by the mouth of Samuel the Prophet, 'I wished you to remain, thou and thy father's house, to offer up incense to the Tabernacle of My Law and to dwell before Me for ever, but now I have repented. I will turn My face away from thee because thou hast treated My offerings with contempt and hath preferred thy sons to Me. And now, him that honoureth Me I will honour, and him that esteemeth Me lightly I will esteem lightly also; and I will destroy all thy seed.'[1] This He said because the Levites had esteemed Him lightly. And say unto him: "Take this covering of Zion and place it in thy sanctuary, and when thou sacrificeth let thy face be towards us, and sacrifice to Jerusalem and the holy Zion; and when thou prayest let thy face be towards Jerusalem."

And Zadok the priest went and gave David the covering of Zion, and he delivered unto him all the commands which Solomon had spoken. And David, the son of Solomon, rejoiced exceedingly and said, when the covering of the Tabernacle of the Law of God was committed to his charge: "This shall be to me My Lady." And his father said unto him: "Verily he rejoiceth over the covering of Zion and he might subjugate all of us if he were not going back to his own country of Ethiopia."

Then they loaded the wagons, the horses and the mules in order to depart, and they set out on their journey and they continued to travel on. And Michael the Archangel marched in front and he spread out his wings and made them to march through the sea as upon dry land, and upon the dry land he cut a path for them and spreading himself out like a cloud over them he hid them from the fiery heat of the sun. And no man hauled his wagon, but whether it was men, horses, mules or loaded camels, each was raised above the ground to the height of a cubit[2]; and all those who rode upon beasts were lifted up along with the beasts to the height of one span of a man. And every one travelled in the wagons

---

[1] I Samuel 2:29-34

[2] Ancient measure of length; the length of the forearm from the elbow to the tip of the middle finger. Equivalent to 18 inches (45.72 cm).

like a ship on the sea when the wind bloweth, like a bat though the air and like an eagle when his body glideth above the wind. Thus did they travel.

50. THE GIFT OF THE CHARIOT OF ZION TO ETHIOPIA

Then they halted by Gaza, the city of the mother of the King, which Solomon the King had given to the Queen of Ethiopia when she came to him. And from there they came in one day to the border of Gebes in Egypt, the name of which is "Mesrin." And when the sons of the warriors of Israel saw that they came in one day a distance of thirteen days march, and that they were not tired, hungry or thirsty, neither man nor beast, and that they all felt that they had drunk and eaten their fill, these sons of the warriors of Israel knew and believed that this thing was from God.

Then they said unto their king: "Let us let down the wagons, for we have come to the waters of Ethiopia. This is the Takkazi[1] which floweth down from Ethiopia and watereth the Valley of Egypt;" and they let down their wagons there, and set up their tents.

Then the sons of the warriors of Israel went and drove away all the people, and they said unto David their King: "We shall now tell thee and reveal unto thee a secret matter. . . The sun descended from heaven and was given on Sinai to Israel, and it became the salvation of the race of Adam from Moses to the seed of Jesse and behold, it is now with thee by the Will of God. It is not through us that this hath been done, but by the Will of God. . . by the Will of Him that fashioned it and made it, hath this happened. *And now God hath chosen thee to be the servant of the holy and heavenly Zion, the Tabernacle of the Law of God; and it shall be a guide to thee for ever, to thee and to thy seed after thee. For thou wilt not be able to take it back even if thou wishest, and thy father cannot seize it, for it goeth of its own free will, and it cannot be removed from its place if it doth not desire it.* And behold, it is our salvation, our fortress and our place of refuge, our glory and the shelter of our safety.

---

[1]The river Nile

When Azariah had said this, King David was perturbed and he said: "Hast thou in truth, O Lord, remembered us in Thy Mercy... we the castaways, the people whom Thou hast rejected, so that I may see Thy pure habitation which is in heaven, the holy and heavenly Zion? How shall we thank the Lord in return for all the good things which He hath done for us? He hath crowned us with His grace so that we may know upon earth His praise and may serve Him according to His greatness. For He is the Good One to His chosen ones, and unto Him belongeth praise for ever."

Then King David rose up and skipped about like a young sheep and like a kid of the goats that had sucked milk in abundance from his mother, even as his grandfather David rejoiced before the Tabernacle of the Law of God.[1]

He smote the ground with his feet and uttered cries of joy with his mouth... and great joy and gladness were in the camp of the King of Ethiopia. They struck the ground with their feet like young bulls; they clapped their hands together and marvelled; then stretching their hands up to heaven they cast themselves down with their faces to the ground and they gave thanks unto God in their hearts.

51. HOW THE PEOPLE OF ETHIOPIA REJOICED

And King David II (Menyelek I) came and stood up before Zion and he saluted it and made obeisance unto Zion, and said: "O Lord God of Israel, to thee be praise, because Thou doest Thy Will and not the will of men. Thou makest the wise man to forget his wisdom, and Thou destroyest the counsel of the counsellor. Thou raisest the poor man from the depth and Thou settest the sole of his foot upon a strong rock. For a full cup of glory is in Thy hand for those who love Thee, and a full cup of shame for those who hate Thee. As for us, our salvation shall go forth from Zion and He shall remove sin from His people, and goodness and mercy shall be poured out in all the world. For we are the work of His hands, and who shall rebuke us if He loveth us as Israel His people?

---

[1] II Samuel 6:14-19

And who shall reprove Him if He raiseth us to heaven and His throne? For death and life are from Him, and glory and dishonour are in His hand; He hath the power to punish or to multiply His compassion."

After this, King David pondered, and said: "Behold Zion, behold salvation, behold the one who rejoiceth, the one adorned with splendour like the sun, behold the one decorated like a bride, not with the apparel of fleeting glory, but the one decorated with the glory and praise which are from God, for thou art the habitation of the God of heaven, the Lord of armies."

Thus spake David the King, Son of Solomon, King of Israel. *For the Spirit of Prophecy descended upon him because of his joy,* and he knew not what he said and he was like Peter and John on the top of Mount Tabar. And they all marvelled and said: "This, the son of a prophet, is to be numbered among the prophets!"

And the people of Ethiopia took flutes and blew horns, they beat drums and played on pipes, and the river of Egypt was moved and astonished at the sound of their songs and their rejoicings; and with them were mingled shouts and outcries of gladness. Then the idols which they had made with their hands and were in the forms of men, dogs, cats and high towers, also the figures of birds of gold and silver, they all fell down and were broken in pieces. For Zion shone like the sun, and at her majesty they were dismayed. Then they arrayed Zion in her apparel and they bore gifts before her, set her upon her chariot, spread out purple beneath her and they draped her richly and sang songs around her.

Then the wagons rose up and they set out early in the morning, and the people sang songs to Zion and they were all raised up the space of a cubit, and as the people of the country of Egypt bade them farewell, they passed before them like shadows, and those people worshipped them for they saw Zion moving in the heavens like the sun, and they all ran with the chariot of Zion, some in front and some behind her.

Then they came to Al-Ahmar which is in Eritrea at the Red Sea, the same which was divided by the hand of Moses and the children of Israel marched in the depths of it as on dry land. At that time the Tabernacle of the Law of God had not been given unto Moses, and therefore the water only gathered itself together, a wall on the right hand and a wall on the left, and allowed Israel to pass with their beasts and their children and their wives. After they had crossed the sea God spoke to Moses and gave him the Tabernacle of the Covenant with the Book of the Law.

When holy Zion crossed over with those who were in attendance and who sang songs to the music of harps and flutes, the sea received them and its waves leaped up and roared as a lion roareth when he is enraged, and it thundered as the winter thunder of Damascus and Ethiopia when the lightning striketh the clouds. The sea worshipped Zion, and their wagons were raised above the waves for a space of three cubits.

And there was joy at the sea of Eritrea, and the people of Ethiopia who went forth to the sea rejoiced exceedingly, with a greater joy than did Israel when they came out of Egypt. When they arrived opposite Mount Sinai and dwelt in Kades, they remained there while the angels sang praises and the creatures of the spirit-world mingled their praises with the children of earth, with songs, psalms and tambourines, joyfully.

Again they loaded their wagons and they rose up and departed, and journeyed on to the land of Medyam, and came to the country of Belontos which is a Kingdom of Ethiopia. Then they encamped there because they had reached the border of their country with glory and joy, without tribulation on the way, in a wagon of the spirit by the night of heaven and of Michael the Archangel. And all the provinces of Ethiopia rejoiced, for Zion sent forth a light like that of the sun into the darkness wherever she went.

52. ZADOK THE PRIEST DISCOVERS THAT THE TABERNACLE OF ZION HAS DISAPPEARED

When Zadok the priest returned to Solomon the King, he found him sorrowful. And the King said unto Zadok the priest: "When the Queen came, there appeared to me by night this vision: It seemed as if I were standing in the chamber of Jerusalem and the sun came down from heaven into the land of Judah, and lighted it up with great splendour and having tarried a time it went down and lighted up the country of the Negus, Ethiopia, and it did not return to the land of Judah. And again the sun came down from heaven to the country of Judah and lighted it up more brilliantly than it did the first time, but the Israelites paid no heed to it, and they plotted to extinguish its light. But it rose below the earth in a place where it was not expected, and it shined upon the country of Rome and the country of Ethiopia, and afterwards upon all those who believed on it."

Zadok the priest answered and said unto him: "O my Lord, why didst thou not tell me before that thou hadst seen a vision of this kind? Thou makest my knees to tremble. Woe be unto us if our sons have carried off our Lady, the holy, heavenly Zion, the Tabernacle of the Law of God!" And the King answered and said unto him: "Our wisdom is forgotten and our understanding is buried. Verily the sun that appeared unto me long ago when I was sleeping with the Queen of Ethiopia is the symbol of the holy Zion. But tell me, yesterday when thou didst take off the splendid covering that was lying upon Zion, didst thou make certain that Zion was there?" Zadok the priest answered and said: "I did not Lord; it had three coverings over it, and I took off the outermost one, and dressed Zion in the covering which thou gave to me, and I brought the other one to thee." King Solomon then said unto Zadok: "Go quickly and look at our Lady Zion and examine her closely." Zadok the priest took the keys and went and opened the house of the sanctuary, and he examined quickly, but he found there nothing except the wooden boards which Azariah had fastened together and had made to resemble the sides of Zion.

When Zadok saw this he fell forward on his face flat upon the ground, and his spirit was poured out from him, for he was terrified and became like a dead man. When he tarried in coming out, Solomon sent Benaiah to seek him, and he found Zadok like dead. Benaiah then lifted up the head of Zadok and felt for his heart and his nose to find out whether there was any sign of life in him, and he fanned him, lifted him up, rubbed him and laid him out upon a table. Then Zadok rose up and looked at the place where Zion had been set, and he found her not, and he again fell down upon the ground, and he cast dust upon his head, rose up and went out and wailed at the doors of the house of God; and the sound of his cries was heard as far as the King's palace.

King Solomon then rose up and commanded the herald to cry out and the soldiers to blow the trumpets so that the people might go forth and pursue the men of the land of Ethiopia, and if they overtook them they were to seize his son and bring him back with the Tabernacle Zion, and slay all the other men with the sword. For with his mouth he spoke thus: "As the Lord God of Israel liveth, they are men of death and not of life; for verily they deserve death because they have robbed the house of the sanctuary of God, and have desired to pollute the habitation of His Name in a land wherein there is not His Law."

53. HOW SOLOMON ROSE UP TO SLAY THEM

Thus spoke King Solomon. And the King rose up in wrath and set out to pursue the men of Ethiopia. When the King and his nobles and his mighty men of war rose up, the elders of Israel, the widows and the virgins gathered together in the house of God and they wept bitterly for Zion, for the Tabernacle of the Law of God had been taken from them.

Then the King commanded that the soldiers should go forth on the right and on the left, on the chance that some of the fugitives might turn aside through fear of the theft. And the King himself rose up and followed the track of the men on the road to Ethiopia, and he sent out mounted horsemen so that they might go ahead of him to find out where they were, and return and bring him news of them.

The horsemen journeyed on and came to the country of Egypt where the men of Ethiopia had encamped with their king. The soldiers of King Solomon questioned the people, and the men of the country of Egypt said unto them: "Some days ago certain men of Ethiopia passed here; they travelled swiftly in wagons, like the angels, and they were swifter than the eagles of the heavens." Then the King's soldiers said unto him: "How many days ago is it since they left you?" And the men of Egypt said unto them: "This day is the ninth day since they left us." And some of the King's horsemen who returned said unto King Solomon: "Nine days have passed since they left Egypt. Some of our companions have gone to seek for them at the Sea of Eritrea, but we came back so that we might report this to thee, O King. On the third day after they went forth they arrived at the river Takkazi in the land of Egypt; and we, being sent forth by thee from Jerusalem, arrived on the day of the Sabbath. Now we came back to thee today, the fourth day of the week. Consider in thy wisdom the distance which those men have travelled." The King was angry and said: "Seize the five of them, until we find out the truth of their words."

King Solomon and his soldiers marched quickly and they came to Gaza where the King asked the people: "When did my son leave you?" And they answered and said unto him: "He left us three days ago, and after loading their wagons none of them travelled on the ground, but their wagons were suspended in the air; they were swifter than the eagles that are in the sky, and all their baggage travelled with them in wagons above the winds. As for us, we thought that thou, in thy wisdom had made them to travel in wagons above the winds."

Then the King said unto them: "Was Zion, the Tabernacle of the Law of God, with them?" And they said unto him: "We did not see anything."

54. SOLOMON ARRIVES IN EGYPT

When King Solomon left that place he met one of the nobles of Egypt whom King Pharaoh had sent unto him with gifts; there was an abundance of treasures with him, and he came and made obeisance to the King. And Solomon the King made haste to question him even before he had presented his gift and credentials, and said unto him: "Hast thou seen men of Ethiopia fleeing by this route?" The ambassador of Pharaoh answered and said unto the King: "O King, live forever! My Lord, King Pharaoh sent me unto thee from Alexandria, and then I came to Cairo the city of the King, and on my arrival there, these men of Ethiopia of whom thou speakest arrived there also. They reached there after a passage of three days on the Takkazi, the river of Egypt, and they were blowing flutes, and they travelled on wagons like the host of the heavenly beings. And those who saw them said: 'These, having once been creatures of earth, have become beings of heaven.' Who then is wiser than Solomon the King of Judah? But he never travelled in this manner in a wagon of the winds. And those who were in the cities and towns were witnesses that when these men came into the land of Egypt, our gods and the gods of the King fell down and were dashed in pieces, and the towers of the idols were likewise broken into fragments. And they asked the priests of the gods, the diviners of Egypt, the reason why our gods had fallen down, and they said unto us: 'The Tabernacle of the God of Israel, which came down from heaven, is with them and will abide in their country forever.' And it was because of this, when they came into the land of Egypt our gods were broken into fragments.

And thou O King, whose wisdom hath no counterpart under the heavens, why hast thou given away the Tabernacle of the Law of the Lord thy God, which thy father kept pure for thee? For, according to what we hear, that Tabernacle used to deliver you out of the hand of your enemies, and the Spirit of Prophecy, which was therein, used to hold converse with you, and the God of heaven dwells in it in His Holy Spirit, and ye are called men of the house of God. Why have ye given your glory to another?" Solomon answered in his wisdom and said: "How was David able to carry away our Lady Zion, for she is with us?"

55. SOLOMON'S LAMENT FOR THE TABERNACLE OF ZION

Solomon entered into his tent and wept bitterly, and said: "O God, hast Thou taken away the Tabernacle of Thy Covenant from us in my days? If only Thou hadst taken away my life before this which Thou hast taken away in my days! For Thou cannot make Thy word to be a lie, and Thou cannot break Thy Covenant which Thou didst make with our fathers, with Noah Thy servant who kept righteousness, with Abraham who did not transgress Thy commandment, and with Isaac Thy servant who kept his body pure from the pollution of sin... with Israel Thy holy one, whom Thou didst call 'Thy people Israel,' and with Moses and Aaron Thy priests, in whose days Thou didst make the Tabernacle of the Law to come down from heaven upon earth, to the children of Jacob Thine inheritance, with Thy Law and Thy Commandments in the form of the constitution of the angels. For Thou hadst already made Zion as the habitation of Thy glory upon the mountain of Thy sanctuary. And again Thou didst give it to Moses that he might serve it nobly upon the earth and might make it to dwell in the 'Tent of Witness' so that Thou Thyself mightest come there from the mountain of Thy sanctuary and make the people to hear Thy voice so that they might walk in Thy Commandments.

Now I know that Thou regardest Thine inheritance more lightly than Thy people Israel. Until this time it was with us and we did not minister unto it correctly, and for this reason Thou art angry with us and Thou hast turned Thy face from me. O Lord, look not upon our evil deeds, but consider Thou the goodness of our forefathers.

My father David, Thy servant, wished to build a house to Thy Name, for he had heard the word of Thy prophet who said: 'Which is the house for my habitation, and which is the place for Me to rest in? Is it not My hands that have made all this, saith the Lord[1] Who ruleth everything?' It is impossible for thee to build this, but he who hath gone forth from thy loins shall build a house for me.[2] And now, O Lord, Thy word hath not been made a lie, and I have built Thy house, Thou being my guide. And when I had finished building Thy house, I brought the Tabernacle of the Covenant into it, and I offered up sacrifices to Thy most holy Name, and Thou didst look on these kindly. And the house was full of Thy glory, the whole world being filled with Thy Godhead, and we Thy people rejoiced at the sight of Thy glory therein.

This day it is three days since that time, and Thou hast snatched away Thy light from us that Thou mayest shine upon those that are in darkness. Thou hast removed our honour that Thou mayest honour those who are unworthy; Thou hast blotted out our majesty that Thou mayest make majestic him that is not majestic; Thou hast taken away our life that Thou mayest build up him whose life is far from Thee.

Woe is me! I weep for myself. Rise up David, my father, and weep with me for our Lady Zion, for God hath neglected us and hath taken away our Lady from thy son. Woe is me! Woe is me! For the sun of righteousness

---

[1]Isaiah 66:1   [2]I Corinthians 22:8-9

hath neglected me. Woe is me! For we have neglected the command of our God, and we have become rejected ones on the earth. As priests we have not acted well, and as kings we have not done what is right in respect of justice to the orphan. Woe be unto us! What is holy hath passed from us, and we are rebuked.

Our joy hath turned away to our enemies, and the grace that was ours hath been removed from us. Our back is turned towards the spears of our enemies. Woe be unto us! Our children have become the spoil and captives of those whom we recently had spoiled and made captives. Our widows weep and our virgins mourn. Woe be unto us ! Our old men wail and our young men lament. Our women shed tears and our city is laid waste. From this day to the end of our days we shall mourn, and our children likewise, for the glory of the daughter of Zion is removed, and the glory of the daughter of Ethiopia, hath increased.

God is angry, and who shall show compassion? God hath made unclean, and who shall purify? God hath planned, and who shall overrule His plan? God speaketh, and everything shall come to pass. God hath taken away, and there is none who shall bring back. Our name was honoured, and today it is nothing. From being men of the household of God, we have become men of the outside, and from being men of the inner chambers we have been driven out through our sins. For God loveth the pure, but the priests would have none of the pure, and have loved the impure.

The prophets rebuked us, but we would not accept admonition, and they wanted to make us hear, but we would not hear. Woe be unto us! Through our sins we are rejected and because of our apostasy we shall be punished. Sovereignty profiteth nothing without purity, and judgment profiteth nothing without justice, and riches profit nothing without the fear of God. The priests love the words of fables more than the words of the scriptures; and they love the sound of the harp more than the sound of the Psalter[1]; they love the praises of men more than prayer; and they love laughter and fornication more than the trials of life; they love wine and drink more than sacrificing to God. They love idleness more than prayer; they love to possess more than to give; and

[1]The Book of Psalms

they love sleeping more than praising, dozing more than watching. Woe be unto us!

O Zion, we have been negligent in respect of the Commandment of God. We have loved the words of the fablemongers more than the words of the priests. We have wished to gaze upon the face of our women rather than upon the face of God in repentance. We have loved the word of foolishness more than the words of the wise, and we have loved the words of fools more than the words of the Prophets. Of our own free will we have polluted our life. The repentance and mercy which God loveth we have not done. He gave us glory and we have thrown it away; He made us very wise, and of our own free will we have made ourselves more foolish than the beasts. We have preferred the luxuriousness of food, which becometh dung, to the food of life which endureth for ever. Our governors and the people do what God hateth, and they love not what God loveth; love for their neighbours and meekness, graciousness, mercy for the poor, patient endurance and love of the house of God.

But what God hateth is idolatry, divination, magic and enquiry of witches, theft, oppression, fornication, envy, drunkenness, false swearing and the bearing of false testimony.

All these things which God hateth we have done. And it is because of these that God hath taken away the Tabernacle of His Covenant from us and hath given it to the people who do His Will and His Law. He hath turned His face from us and hath made His face to shine upon them. He hath despised us and hath loved them; He hath shown mercy unto them and hath blotted us out. For He hath sworn an oath by Himself that He will not take away winter and summer, seed time and halvest, fruit and work, sun and moon, as long as Zion is on the earth, and that He will not in wrath destroy heaven and earth, either by flood or fire, and that He will not blot out man, beast, reptiles and creeping things, but will show mercy to the work of His hands, and will multiply His mercy on what He hath formed. But when God taketh away the Tabernacle of His Covenant He will destroy the heavens and the earth, and all His work; and this day hath God despised us and taken from us the Tabernacle of His Law."

As Solomon was saying these things he ceased not to weep, and the tears ran down his cheeks continually.

Then the Spirit of Prophecy answered and said unto him: "Why art thou sorrowful? For this hath happened by the Will of God. And Zion hath not been given to an alien... *but to thy firstborn son who shall sit upon the throne of David thy father.*

For God swore unto David in truth, and he repenteth not, that of the fruit of his body He would make to sit upon his throne forever, in the Tabernacle of His Covenant, the holy Zion. And I will set him above the kings of the earth, *and His throne shall be like the days of heaven and like the ordinance of the moon forever.[1] And He Who sitteth upon the throne of the Godhead in the heavens shall rule the living and the dead in the flesh forever.*

And angels and men shall serve Him, and every tongue shall praise Him, and every knee shall bow to Him in the heavens and upon the earth. Comfort thyself with this word and get back to thy house, and let not thy heart be sad."

The King was comforted by these words and he said: "The Will of God be done, and not the will of man." And again the Angel of God appeared unto him openly, and said unto him: "As for thyself, thou shalt build the house of God, and it shall be glory and support for thee; and if thou keep His Commandment and serve not other gods thou shalt be beloved by God, even as David thy father."

56. SOLOMON'S RETURN TO JERUSALEM

When Solomon came back to the city of Jerusalem, he wept there with the elders of Jerusalem, a great weeping in the house of God. And after this the King and Zadok the priest embraced each other, and wept bitterly in the habitation of Zion, then they remained silent for a long time. Eventually the elders rose up and spoke unto the King, saying:

---

[1] II Samuel 7:8-17

"Be not thou sorrowful concerning this thing, Our Lord, for we know, from first to last, that without the Will of God Zion will not dwell anywhere and that nothing happens without the Will of God.

Concerning Zion in olden times, in the days of Eli the priest, before our fathers had asked for a king, the Philistines carried away the Tabernacle of the Law of God and brought it into their city, and set it in the house of their god Dagon. And Dagon was broken to pieces and destroyed, and became like dust. Their land became a desert through mice which ate up all the fruit of their land and the people suffered boils and sores.

The Philistines then gathered together their priests, magicians and stargazers, and they said unto them: 'How can we relieve ourselves of these sores and the tribulations which have come upon us, and upon our country?' And those magicians meditated and withdrew themselves to be alone, and they brought their magical instruments, and pondered and considered, and planned how they could relieve them from the tribulation of their city and their persons. They discovered that this punishment had come upon them and their city because of Zion.

Then they went to their kings and their governors, and they said unto them: 'All things have befallen you through the heavenly Zion, the Tabernacle of the Law of God. And now, this is how ye will take her back into her city, and her country and her house. By no means send her away empty, but give her an offering so that she may forgive you your sins, and cast away your tribulations when she is returned to her city. But if ye will not send her back to her city, no good will come by forcing her to live with you, but ye shall continue to be punished until ye are destroyed.'

The king and the governors then said unto their priests: 'What gift ought we to give her, and how shall we send her back? Find out and tell us what we must do.' And the priests of the Philistines took counsel together again, and they said unto their king and unto their governors: 'Make for her according to the heads of your houses, sixty images of mice in gold, since mice have destroyed our land, and sixty images of the member of a man, since your own persons have suffered from sores and boils on your members.'[1]

---

[1] I Samuel, Chapters 4, 5, 6

79

And the Philistines made as they commanded them one hundred and twenty offerings of gold, and gave them to Zion. And again the magicians of the Philistines said unto them: "Let them bring two she-camels[1] that brought forth their firstborn at the same time, and let them attach a chariot[2] to them. Keep back their young ones and shut them up in the house; then yoke the two she-camels together and set them free and let them go where they will. If they march straight for Jerusalem we shall know that God hath had compassion on our land; but if they wander about, and wish to return to the place whence they started, then we shall know that God is still wroth with us, and that he will not remove His punishment until He hath blotted out ourselves and our city."

The Philistines did as the priests commanded their governors, and they sent away Zion, and prostrated themselves before her. And those camels made their way straight to the country of Judah, and they came to the threshing floor and the house of thy people did receive them. But those who did not receive them were the men of the house of Dan, and they did not do homage to Zion for they regarded her in anger as their desecrated God.

So they cut up the pieces of wood of the wagon and made those camels to be sacrifice, but Zion returned to her place, and whilst Zion was in her house Samuel the Prophet ministered unto her, and vision and prophecy were revealed unto him, and he pleased God in all his actions, and he ruled Israel for forty-eight years.

After him our people entreated God to give them a king like the nations that were round about them. And Samuel the Prophet anointed Saul the king, and he reigned forty years; he was of the tribe of Benjamin, which was the youngest branch of the peoples of Israel. Samuel the Prophet also anointed thy father David and when the Philistines fought with Saul the king, Saul was conquered and died with Jonathan his son.

Those of Saul's sons who were left wished to carry away Zion, when they knew that their father and their brother were dead. And then when they wished to hide her and to transfer her to the valley of Gilboa in order that thy father David might not carry her off, she would not let

---

[1] I Samuel 6:7-12 [2] I Samuel 6:7

them carry her away until thy father came and carried her away from their city, but not with offerings nor with incense and burnt offerings. For it was impossible to carry Zion away unless she wished it and God wished it.

And again, when thy father reigned over Israel, he took her from the city of Samaria and brought her here to Jerusalem, dancing on his feet before her, and clapping his hands because of joy for her; for she was taken by him so that she might come to the city of David thy father.

As for that which thou sayest concerning the going of Zion to the country of Ethiopia, if God willed it, there is no one who could prevent it; for of her own will she went, and of her own will she will return if God pleaseth. And if she does not return it will be God's good pleasure... and as for us, if God hath willed it Jerusalem shall remain to us wherein thou hast built for us a house of God.

So now, let not thine heart be sad, but comfort thyself with what we have said unto thee; and the wisdom which the Lord God of Israel hath given thee, hath sprouted from thee. For wisdom is a strange thing. As a lamp is not the sun, and as vinegar and aloes are neither profitable nor useful additions to honey, even so the words of fools are not beneficial to the wise man. And as smoke is to the eye, and an unripe fruit to the tooth, even so the words of fools are not beneficial to the wise."

57. THE ELDERS OF ISRAEL KEEP THE DEPARTURE OF ZION A SECRET

Solomon the King answered and said unto them: "Hearken ye unto me and unto what I shall say unto you: Supposing He had taken me away whilst I was carrying Zion, what is impossible to God? And supposing He were to make them to inherit our city, and destroy us; what is impossible to God? For everything is His and none can overcome His Will, and there is none who can oppose His command in heaven above or on earth below. He is the King Whose kingdom shall never, never pass away. But now let us go and kneel in the House of God."

And the elders of Israel together with their King went into the House of God, and they entered the Holy of Holies, and they made supplication and prostrated themselves, and ascribed blessing to God.

Then Solomon wept in the habitation of the heavenly Zion, the Tabernacle of the Law of God, and they all wept with him, and after a little while they held their peace. King Solomon then said unto them: "Cease ye, so that the uncircumcised people may not boast themselves over us, and say: 'Their glory is taken away, and God hath forsaken them.' *Reveal ye not anything else to alien folk.* Let us set up these boards which are here nailed together, and let us cover them over with gold, and let us decorate them after the manner of our Lady Zion, and let us lay the Book of the Law inside it.

Jerusalem, the free, that is in the heavens above us, which Jacob our father saw, is with us, and below it is the Gate of Heaven, this Jerusalem on earth. If we do the Will of God and His good pleasure, God will be with us and will deliver us out of the hand of our enemy, and out of the hand of all those who hate us... God's Will and not our will be done.

Through this He hath made us sorrowful. From now on, His wrath will cool in respect of us, and He will not abandon us to our enemies, and He will not remove His mercy far from us; He will remember the covenant with our fathers Abraham, and Isaac and Jacob. He will not make His word to be a lie, and will not break His Covenant so that our father's seed be destroyed."

And then the elders of Israel answered and said unto him: "May thy good pleasure be done, and the good pleasure of the Lord God! As for us, none of us will transgress thy word, *and we will not inform any other people that Zion hath been taken away from us." And they established this covenant in the House of God the elders of Israel with King Solomon unto this day.* And Solomon lived for eleven years after the taking away of Zion from him, and then his heart turned aside from the love of God, and he forgot his wisdom, through his excessive love of women.

Solomon loved greatly the daughter of Pharaoh the king of Egypt, whose name was Makshara, and he brought her into the house which he had made. In the roof thereof, there were figures of the sun, moon and stars, and it was illumined by night as brightly as by day. Its beams were made of brass and its roof of silver; and its floor was of blocks of sapphire stone and sardius, with its walls of lead and red and black stones. He used to go and dwell therein through his love for his house and for his wife Makshara, the daughter of Pharaoh, King of Egypt.

Queen Makshara possessed certain idols which her father had given her to bow down before, and because when Solomon saw her sacrificing to them and worshipping them, he did not rebuke her or forsake her, God was wroth with him and made him to forget his wisdom. But she multiplied her sacrifices and her worship, also her folly according to the stupidity of the Egyptians... and all the people of her house worshipped the statues and learned the foolish service of idols. Enjoying the pleasure of their ignorance, they worshipped with the daughter of Pharaoh, and the children of Israel joined themselves unto that woman and her handmaidens in the worship of idols.

Solomon himself found pleasure hearing their folly. And when she saw that he loved her and held his peace, and asked many questions about the gods of the Egyptians, she made herself exceedingly agreeable to him, and she spoke to him with honeyed words, with the tender speech of women and the sweet smile that goes with the doing of an evil deed, with the turning of the face and the assumption of a look of good intent, and with the nodding of the head.

With actions of this kind she caused his heart to turn away from his God, and she enticed him to the evil of her work, wishing to drag him down into the folly of the foolish service of idols. And as the deep sea draweth down into its depths the man who cannot swim, until the water overwhelms him and destroys his life, even so did that woman wish to submerge Solomon the King.

The Ark of the Covenant, The Tabernacle of the Law of God, The Ark of Testimony, The Holy Ark, Zion, Lady Zion, Ark of God.

"And thou shalt put the Ark-cover above upon the Ark; and in the Ark thou shalt put the testimony that I shall give thee. And there I shall meet with thee and I will speak with thee above the Ark-cover, from between the two cherubim which are upon the Ark of the Testimony, of all things which I will give thee in commandment unto the Children of Israel." (Exodus 25:21-22)

(Specially commissioned artistic conception, by David Clayton.)

Makeda, Queen of Sheba

Also known as Candace, Queen of Ethiopia... Queen of the South, called
Balkis by the Arabs. (Authorised Version/King James, 1611, dedicates
only 13 and 12 verses respectively to her visit to Jerusalem in 992 B.B.
See 1 Kings 10: 1-13 and II Chronicles 9: 1-12).

Specially commissioned artistic conception, by David Clayton

MUSLIM DOME OF THE ROCK MOSQUE
(Muslim Shrine), Jerusalem

The third most holy site of the Muslim faith, built over the exact spot where Solomon's temple stood on Temple Mount (Mount Moriah) during the rule of the Omayyad Caliphs (660-750 AD). Of the 36 mosques now in Jerusalem, the Dome of the Rock Mosque is at the centre of an historic-religious controversy with the Jewish faith. Built over the spot where the Prophet Mohammed was presumably caught up to heaven, it is the only location where the Temple of God can be erected again.

Courtesy, Embassy of Israel, Kingston, Jamaica

THE WESTERN WALL or 'WAILING WALL'

Last remaining vestige of the Herodian Temple in Jerusalem (Second Temple). Destroyed in 70 AD by the Roman legions under General Titus, the Second Temple was inferior to the First (Solomonic) Temple because of the absence of the Ark of the Covenant. Today it is a centre of Jewish worship and lamentation in remembrance of Israel's glorious past, and a rallying point for those who look forward to the rebuilding of the Holy Temple and the re-establishment of Israel's biblical grandeur.

OPERATION MOSES
(1984)
Rescue of the Ethopian Jews

*"And I will bring you in unto
the land... and I will give it
you for an heritage: I am the
Lord." (Exodus 6:8)*

*"...They are thy people and
thine inheritance, which thou
broughtest out by thy mighty
power and by thy
stretched out arm."
(Deuteronomy 9:29)*

*(Photos, courtesy Embassy of Israel,
Kingston, Jamaica)*

The Dominions of David and Solomon

PART IV

The Fall of Israel

When the chief priests therefore and officers saw him, they cried out, saying Crucify him, crucify him.

John 19.6

58. HOW THE DAUGHTER OF PHARAOH SEDUCED SOLOMON

Then the daughter of Pharaoh appeared before Solomon and said unto him: "It is good to worship the gods like my father and all the kings of Egypt who were before my father did." Solomon answered and said unto her: "They call gods the things which have been made by the hands of the worker in metal, by the carpenter, the potter, the painter, the sculptor... these are not gods, but the work of the hand of man, in gold, silver, stone, lead, iron and clay... and ye call 'our gods' the things that are not gods. But we worship none else than the Holy God of Israel and our Lady, the holy and heavenly Zion, the Tabernacle of the Law of God, whom He hath given us to worship, we and our seed after us."

And she answered and said unto him: *"Thy son hath carried away Zion, thy son whom thou hast begotten, who springeth from an alien people into which God hath not commanded you to marry, from an Ethiopian woman, who is not of thy colour, not akin to thy country, and who is, moreover, black."*

And Solomon answered and said unto her: "Art thou not thyself of that race concerning which God hath not commanded us that we should take wives from? And thy race is her race, for ye are all the children of Ham.[1] And God, having destroyed of the seed of Ham seven kings, hath made us to inherit this city, that we and our seed after us may dwell therein for ever. As concerning Zion, the will of God hath been performed, and He hath given her unto them so that they may worship her. As for me, I will neither worship nor sacrifice to thine idols, and I will not perform thy wish."

One day she beautified and scented herself for him, and she behaved herself haughtily towards him and treated him disdainfully. And he said unto her: "What shall I do? Thou hast made thy face evil towards me, and not as it was before, and thy beautiful form is not as enticing as usual. Ask me, and I will give thee whatsoever thou wishest, and I will perform it for thee, so that thou mayest make thy face gracious towards me as former," but she held her peace and answered him not a word.

---

[1]Genesis 5:32, 9:20-27

And he repeated to her the words that he would do whatsoever she wished. And then she said unto him: "Swear to me by the God of Israel."

He swore to her that he would give her whatsoever she asked for, and that he would do for her everything that she told him. And she tied a scarlet thread on the middle of the door of the temple of her gods, and she brought three locusts and set them in the house of her gods. And she said unto Solomon: "Come to me without breaking the scarlet thread, bend thyself and kill these locusts before me and pull out their heads." And he did so. And she said unto him: "I will henceforward do thy will, for thou hast sacrificed to my gods and hast worshipped them." He had done thus because of his oath so that he might not break his oath which she had made him to swear, even though he knew that it was a sin to enter into the house of her gods.

God had commanded the children of Israel, saying: "Ye shall not marry strange women, that ye may not be corrupted by them through their gods, and through the wickedness of their works and the sweetness of their voices; for they make so the hearts of simple young men by the sweetness of their gentle voices, and by the beauty of their forms they destroy the wisdom of the foolish man." Who was wiser than Solomon? Yet he was seduced by a woman. Who was more righteous than David? Yet he was seduced by a woman. Who was handsomer than Amnon? Yet he was seduced by Tamar the daughter of David his father.[1] And Adam was the first creation of God, yet he was seduced by Eve his wife; and through that seduction death came for every created being.

59. THE SIN OF SOLOMON

Solomon sinned an exceedingly great sin through the worship of idols, and from being a wise man he became a fool, and his sin is written down in the Books of the Prophets... but God had mercy on Solomon for this error which is written down as his sin, and his name is numbered with Abraham, Isaac, Jacob and David his father in the book of life in heaven. For God is a forgiver of those who have sinned. Which was the

---

[1] II Samuel 3:2; I Chronicles 3:1

greater of the two, the sin of his father David or the sin of his son Solomon? David caused Uriah to be slain in battle by means of a plan of deceit so that he might take his wife Bathsheba, who became the mother of Solomon; but he repented and God had compassion on him.

60. CONCERNING THE PROPHECY OF CHRIST

According to the interpretation of prophecy, the name Solomon signifieth in the secret speech "Christ." Solomon built the house of God, and Christ raised up His body and made it into the Church. And when He said unto the Jews: "Throw down this house, and in three days I will build it up again."[1] He was speaking to them of the house of His Body.

And as Solomon multiplied wives from alien peoples because of their beauty and winsomeness, and desires arose in him because of his love for them, so Christ gathered together from alien peoples those who had not the Law, but who believed on Him. And there was no uncircumcised man to him, no pagan, no slave, no Jew, no servant and no free man;[2] but he gathered them all into His heavenly kingdom by His Flesh and Blood.

In the Song of Songs, Solomon himself sang and said: "There are sixty mighty men round about the bed of Solomon, all of them trained in war and holding swords, each man with his sword upon his thigh."[3] The number sixty indicateth the number of righteous Patriarchs, the Prophets, Apostles, Martyrs, Believers and Saints who have resisted the war of Satan.

The word "sword" is, being interpreted, the word of the Scriptures. The word of the Lord cutteth like a straight, sharp sword, and in like manner the Scriptures cut from men's hearts the danger caused by deceitful fables and imaginings.

Again Solomon sang, saying: "King Solomon hath made a chariot for himself,"[4] and these words are to be interpreted that Christ did put on

---

[1] John 2:19   [2] Galatians 3:28   [3] Songs of Solomon 3:7-8
[4] Songs of Solomon 3:9

our body. The name Solomon in the language of the Hebrews is, being interpreted, "Christ." And the foolish Jews imagine that the words of David: "The Lord said unto me, 'Thou art my son and this day I have begotten thee',"[1] were spoken concerning Solomon his son.

"O God, give Thy judgment to the King, and Thy righteousness to the son of the King, so that he may judge Thy people with righteousness and Thy needy ones with justice. And he shall live and they shall give him of the gold of Arabia, and shall pray for him continually, and shall follow him with good words, and he shall be a support for the whole earth on the tops of the mountains, and his fruit shall be greater than the cedar, and he shall flourish in the city like the grass of the earth, and his name shall be before the sun.[2] I have brought thee forth from the belly before the Morning Star.[3] God hath sworn, and He will not repent, thou art His priest for ever, after the appointment of Melchizedek."[4]

Concerning this prophecy and others like it, which David prophesied concerning Christ, the foolish Jews who are blind of heart, say that what David said was spoken concerning his son Solomon; this do the Jews say, and they make Christ to be Solomon because of the similarity of name and the wisdom, and because He was the Son of David in the flesh. And although those who came after David and Solomon, namely Elijah and Elisha, knew this, they ascribed Solomon's sin to him in the Book of Kings in order that they might put to shame the Jews, who are binded in heart and are the enemies of righteousness.

Solomon the King, the son of David the King and Prophet, was himself also King and Prophet, and he prophesied many similarities concerning Christ and concerning the Church, and he wrote four books of prophecy, and is numbered with Abraham, Isaac, Jacob and David his father in the Kingdom of the heavens.

61. THE DEATH-LAMENT OF SOLOMON

Solomon was sixty years old when a sickness attacked him. And his days were not as the days of David his father, but they were twenty years shorter than his, because he was under the sway of women and

---

[1]Psalm 2:7   [2]Psalm 72:1-5   [3]Rev. 2:28; 22:16; II Peter 1:19   [4]Psalm 110:4

worshipped idols. And the Angel of Death came and smote him in the foot, and he wept and said: "O Lord God of Israel, I am conquered by the terrestrial law, for there is no one free from blemish before Thee, O Lord, and there is no one righteous and wise before Thee, O Lord. For Thou dost scrutinize and try the heart. Nothing is hidden from Thee. Thou lookest upon the hidden things as if they were revealed and Thou searchest out the heart. Have mercy upon me Lord. And if Thou hast mercy upon the righteous who have not transgressed Thy commandments, what is there wonderful in Thy mercy? But if Thou shouldst show mercy upon me, a sinner, Thy mercy would be a marvellous and gracious thing. And although I have sinned, remember Abraham, Isaac, and Jacob my fathers who did not transgress Thy commandments. Have mercy upon me, Lord, for the sake of David Thy servant.

O Master of the world, and of kings and governors, O Thou who makest fools to be wise, and the wise to be fools, have mercy upon me, Lord." And as he spoke these words tears streamed down his face.

Then the Angel of God went down to him and said unto him: "Hearken thou unto what I shall say unto thee, for the sake of which God hath sent me. From being a wise man thou hast turned thyself into a fool, and from being a rich man thou hast turned thyself into a poor man, and from being a king thou hast turned thyself into a man of no account, through transgressing the commandment of God. The beginning of thy evil was the taking of many wives by thee, for through this thou didst transgress His Law and the ordinance of God which Moses wrote and gave to you, to Israel, that ye should not marry wives from alien peoples but only from your nation and the house of your fathers, that your seed might be pure and holy and that God might dwell with you.

But thou didst hold lightly the Law of God, thinking that thou wast wiser than God, and that thou wouldst get many male children. Ah, but the foolishness of God is wiser than the wisdom of men, and He hath only given thee three sons; the one who carried off thy glory into an alien land, and made the habitation of God to be in Ethiopia; the one who is lame of foot, who shall sit upon thy throne for the people of Israel, he, the son of thy wife Tarbana of the house of Judah; and the one who is the son of a Greek woman, a handmaiden, who in the last days shall destroy Rehoboam and all thy people Israel... and this land shall be his because he believeth in Him that shall come, the Saviour.

Then the tribe of Rehoboam,[1] and those who are left of Israel shall crucify Him that shall come, the Redeemer, and the memory of you shall be blotted out from the earth. For they shall think out a plan which they shall not be able to establish, and He will be wroth with them and blot out the memorial of them.

And as for thee, Joseph the son of Jacob shall be a symbol of thee. For his brethren sold him into the land of Egypt from Syria, the country of Laban, and on his going down into the land of Egypt there arose a famine in all the world. And through his going down he called his people and delivered them from famine and gave them an habitation in the land of Egypt, the name thereof is Goshen. For he himself was king under Pharaoh, King of Egypt.

Similarly, the Saviour Who shall come from thy seed shall set thee free by His coming, and shall bring thee out of Sheol,[2] where until the Saviour cometh thou shalt suffer pain, together with thy fathers; and He will bring thee forth. For from thy seed shall come forth a Saviour Who shall deliver thee, thee, and those who were before thee, and those who shall come after thee, from Adam to His coming in the tribe of Judah, and He shall make thee to go forth from Sheol as Joseph delivered his people from the famine, so also shall the Saviour bring out of Sheol, you who are His people. And as the Egyptians had made the kinsmen of Joseph slaves, so also have the devils made you slaves through the error of worshipping idols.

And as Moses brought his people out of the slavery of Egypt, so shall the Saviour bring you out of the servitude of Sheol. And as Moses wrought ten miracles and plagues before Pharaoh the King, so the Saviour Who shall come from thy seed shall work ten miracles for life before thy people. And as Moses, after he had wrought the miracles, smote the sea and made the people to pass over as on dry land, so the Saviour Who shall come shall overthrow the walls of Sheol and bring thee out. And as Moses drowned Pharaoh and the Egyptians in the Sea

---

[1]The tribe of Judah   [2]The unknown region; Hades; Hell

of Eritrea, so shall the Saviour drown Satan and his devils in Sheol; for the sea is to be interpreted as Sheol (doom), and Pharaoh as Satan, and his hosts of Egyptians as devils.

Then as Moses fed them with manna in the desert without toil, so shall the Saviour feed you with the food of Paradise forever. And as Moses made them to dwell in the desert for forty years without their apparel becoming worn out, or the soles of their feet becoming torn, so the Saviour shall make you to dwell without toil after the Resurrection. And as Joshua brought them into the Land of Promise, so shall the Saviour bring you into the Garden of Delight.

And as Joshua slew the seven kings of Canaan, so shall the Saviour destroy sinners and shut them up in the fortress of Sheol."

62. THE PEARL AND THE SAVIOUR

"And behold, there shall be unto thee a sign that the Saviour shall come from thy seed, and that He shall deliver thee with thy fathers and thy seed after thee by His coming.

Your salvation was created in the belly of Adam in the form of a pearl before Eve.[1] And when He created Eve out of the rib He brought her to Adam, and said unto them: 'Multiply you from the belly of Adam.' The Pearl did not go into Cain or Abel, but into the third that went forth from the belly of Adam, and it entered into the belly of Seth. Then passing from him, that Pearl went into those who were the firstborn, and came to Abraham. And it did not go from Abraham into his firstborn Ishmael, but it tarried and went into Isaac, the pure. And it did not go into his firstborn, the arrogant Esau, but it went into Jacob the lowly one. And it did not enter from him into his firstborn, the erring Reuben, but into Judah, the innocent one... and it did not go forth from Judah until four sinners had been born, but it came to Perez, the patient one.

Then from him this Pearl went into the firstborn until it came into the belly of Jesse, the father of thy father, and then it waited until six men of wrath had been born, and after that it came to the seventh, David, thy

---

[1]"Pearl" or "Seed" Genesis 21:12; 28:14; I John 3:9

innocent and humble father; for God hateth the arrogant and proud, and loveth the innocent and humble.

The Pearl then waited in the loins of thy father until five erring fools had been born, then it came into thy loins because of thy wisdom and understanding. And then the Pearl waited and it did not go into thy firstborn, for those good men of his country neither denied Him nor crucified Him, like Israel thy people... but when they saw Him Who wrought miracles and Who was to be born from the Pearl, they believed on Him when they heard the report of Him.

And the Pearl did not go forth into thy youngest son Adramis... for those good men neither crucified Him nor denied Him when they saw the workings of miracles and wonders by him that was to be born from the Pearl, and afterwards they believed in Him through His disciples.

Now the Pearl, which is to be thy salvation, went forth from thy belly and entered into the belly of thy son Rehoboam, because of the iniquity of Israel thy people, who in their denial and in their wickedness crucified Him. But if He had not been crucified He could not have been your salvation... for He was crucified without sin, and He rose up again without corruption. And for the sake of this He went down to you into Sheol, and tore down its walls, that He might deliver you and bring you out and show mercy upon all of you.

Ye in whose bellies the Pearl shall be carried, shall be saved with your wives and none of you shall be destroyed, from your father Adam unto him that shall come... and from Eve thy mother, the wife of Adam, to Noah and his wife Tarmiza, to Terah and his wife Aminya, unto Abraham and his wife Sarah, to Isaac and his wife Rebecca and to Jacob and his wife and to Yahuda and his bride Tamar, and thy father and his wife Bathsheba and to thyself and Tarbana thy wife, and to Rehoboam thy son and his wife Amisa, and to Jochim thy kinsman, who is to come, and his wife Hanna."

"None of you who shall have carried the Pearl shall be destroyed, whether it be your men or your women... those who shall have carried the Pearl will not be destroyed. For the Pearl shall be carried by the men who shall be righteous, and the women who have carried the Pearl shall not be destroyed, for they shall become pure through that Pearl, for it is holy and pure, and by it they shall be made holy and pure...because for its sake and for the sake of Zion He hath created the whole world.

Zion hath taken up her abode with thy firstborn Menyelek, and she shall be the salvation of the people of Ethiopia for ever; and the Pearl shall be carried in the belly of Rehoboam thy son, and shall be the Saviour of all the world. And when the appointed time hath come this Pearl shall be born of thy seed, for it is exceedingly pure, seven times purer than the sun. And the Redeemer shall come from the seat of His Godhead, and shall dwell upon her, and shall put on her flesh.

I am Gabriel the Angel, the protector of those who shall carry the Pearl from the body of Adam even to the belly of Hanna, so that I may keep from servitude and pollution you wherein the Pearl shall dwell. And Michael hath been commanded to direct and keep Zion wheresoever she goeth, and Uriel shall direct and keep the wood of the thicket[1] which shall be the Cross of the Saviour. And when thy people in their envy have crucified Him, they shall rush upon His Cross because of the multitude of miracles that shall take place through it, and they shall be put to shame when they see its wonders.

In later times a descendant of thy son Adramis shall take the wood of the Cross, the third means of salvation that shall be sent upon the earth. The Angel Michael is with Zion... with Menyelek thy firstborn, who hath taken the throne of David thy father; and I am with the pure Pearl for Him that shall reign for ever, with Rehoboam thy second son... and the Angel Uriel is with thy younger son Adramis. This have I told thee, and thou shalt not make thy heart to be sad because of thine own salvation and that of thy son."

When Solomon had heard these words his strength came back to him on his bed, and he prostrated himself before the Angel of God, and said: "I give thanks unto the Lord, O thou radiant being of the spirit, because thou hast made me to hear words which filleth me with gladness, and because He doth not cut off my soul from the inheritance of my father because of my sin, and my soul shall be with the soul of David my

---

[1]Compare Genesis 22:12-13

father, and with the soul of Abraham, Isaac and Jacob my fathers. As for my children they shall have upon earth three mighty angels to protect them.

Who is like unto God, the Merciful, Who showeth mercy to His handiwork and glorifieth it, Who forgiveth the sins of the sinners and Who doth not blot out the memorial of the penitent? His whole Person is forgiveness and mercy, and to Him belongeth praise."

63. THE CONVERSATION OF SOLOMON WITH THE ANGEL

Then Solomon turned and looked at the Angel, stretched out both his hands, and said: "My Lord, is the coming of the Saviour of which thou speaketh near or far off?" And the Angel answered and said unto him: *"He will come three and thirty generations from thy seed, and will deliver you. But Israel will hate their Saviour and will be envious of Him because He will work signs and miracles before them. And they will crucify Him, and will kill Him, but He shall rise up again and deliver them, for He is merciful to the penitent and good to those who are His chosen ones.* Behold, I tell you plainly that He will not leave in Sheol His people Israel by whom the Pearl hath been carried."

When the Angel of the Lord had spoken these words unto Solomon, he said unto him: "Peace be unto thee." And Solomon answered and said unto him: "My Lord, I beseech thee, I would ask thee one question; be not unheedful of my cry." And the Angel said unto him: "Speak, ask me thy question, and I will make thee to know what I have heard and seen." And Solomon said unto him: "I am grieved because of Israel, His people, whom He hath chosen as His firstborn from among all the ancient tribes of His inheritance; tell me, will they be blotted out after the coming of the Saviour?" And the Angel of God answered him again and said unto him: "Yea, I have told thee that they will crucify the Saviour. *And when they have poured out His blood on the wood of the Cross they shall be scattered all over the world."* And Solomon said: "I weep for my people. Woe to my people who from first to last have always provoked their Creator to wrath. I and those who have been before me are unworthy to have mercy shown unto us because of the evil of our works, for we are a faithless generation. Woe unto those who shall pour out innocent blood and slander a righteous man, and divide his spoil, and who neither believe in His word nor walk in His commandments!

Their judgment is waiting and their error abideth. Great is their punishment for their work is sin and they shall be destroyed by that which they themselves have imagined."

After this, Solomon turned to his son Rehoboam, and said unto him: "O my son, withhold thyself from evil and do the things that are good, so that thou mayest have many days upon earth. And do not bow down to strange gods, and do not worship them, but fear and honour God only, so that thou mayest conquer thy foes and thy adversaries, and mayest inherit the habitation of thy father in the heavens, and eternal life."

And he said unto him: "Write my name in the roll of the book and lay it in the box." Then he said unto Zadok the priest: "Anoint my son and make him king. As my father David, my Lord, made me king whilst he was alive; even so do I make my son Rehoboam king. And his seed shall be the salvation of myself and of my fathers for ever, according to what the Angel of the Lord spoke unto me."

64. THE REIGN OF REHOBOAM

Then Zadok the priest took Rehoboam and made him king, and he anointed him and performed for him whatsoever the Law demanded. And Rehoboam laid a tablet of wood upon the Tabernacle with the name of his father Solomon written upon it, and then they set him upon the king's mule, and said unto him: "All Hail! Long live the royal father!" and the city resounded with cries, and the trumpet was blown. And before Rehoboam could return to his father, Solomon died.

And they laid Solomon in the tomb of his father David, and they mourned for him with great mourning, for there was not found his like in wisdom in those days.

When seven days had passed Rehoboam made the mourning for his father to cease. And the people of Israel gathered themselves together to Rehoboam, and they said unto him: "Lighten for us our labour, for thy father made it very heavy in the hewing of wood, in the dressing of stone, and in making wagons for bringing down cedar wood." And Rehoboam took counsel with the councillors and the elders of the house of the king, and they said unto him: "Answer them graciously, for at this time thou art like a young animal and thy loins are not yet strong. Speak unto them graciously and say unto them: 'I will do for you everything ye wish.' And when thy hand hath gotten power over them, thou can do with thy people what thou wishest."

Rehoboam then drove out the elders and brought in the foolish young men who had been brought up with him, and he took counsel with them, and told them of the message which the House of Israel had sent to him, and what the elders of the house of the king had counselled him to do. And those foolish young men said unto him: "An aged man giveth the counsel of an aged man, the elder giveth the counsel of an elder, but a young man like thyself giveth the counsel of youth. As for these men who are stricken in years, their loins are as tender as those of a young animal that cannot walk. Concerning this matter of which thou speakest... who can dispute the command of our Lord the King!"

Then one of them leaped up into the air before Rehoboam, and another drew his sword while another brandished his spear, and another seized his bow and quiver. Then when they had made an end of their playing they counselled him saying: "O our Lord, may we be with thee, and thou with us! Thy father in his wisdom gave us the sons of the mighty men of Israel who are learned in the art of war, to grow up with thee so that thy kingdom might be strong after him. O, our Lord, show not a timid face to those men, lest they think that thou art weak and not able to make war against them and against thine enemies. For if they see in us an attitude of weakness in word and in deed, we shall be held in contempt by them, and they will not give us gifts, presents, nor slaves or tribute, and thy kingdom will be destroyed.

O King, address them with bold words and speak unto them haughtily, saying: 'In respect of my father ye say in wood and in stone, but I will make you to serve me with chains of iron and with scorpion-whips. For my little finger shall be stronger than the thickest part of my father's body, and my counsel is greater than the counsel of my father who begot me. None shall diminish for you the labour and the forced service, nay, it shall be increased for you in every particular. And if you will not do my command, I will make your cattle my plunder, and your children shall be captives, and my knife of slaughter shall consume you. And I will seize your cities and your fields, your plantations and your wells, your gardens and your fruits... and I will bind your honourable ones in chains of iron, and your riches shall provide food for my servants... your women shall be for the adornment of the house of my nobles. Behold, I will not alter this my decision and will not diminish it... and I will carry it out quickly and will write it down for ever. For the whole of this land was given to David my grandfather for his kingdom, and to my father Solomon after him. And God hath given it to me after my fathers... and I will make you to serve me as ye served them; and now take counsel and obey me'."

Thus did Rehoboam speak also unto the elders of Israel. And the people all rose up together in their full number, and they said: "Get back to your house, O Israel! Have we none else whom we can make king save in the house of Judah and in the house of Benjamin? We will reject their houses and their men, and we will make our king and governor the man whom we wish for and in whom our soul delighteth." And they took up their weapons of war and fled in one body, and came to the city of Samaria of Beth Efrata, where they took counsel. And the house of Israel cast lots among themselves so that they might make king the man whom they chose.

The lot fell on the house of Ephraim, and they chose a man from the house of his father, and made Jeroboam king. And thus was the kingdom separated from Rehoboan the son of Solomon and there were left to it only the house of Benjamin and the house of Judah his father.

He who reigned on the throne of David his father was Jesus Christ, His kinsman in the flesh by a virgin, Who sat upon the throne of His Godhead; and upon earth He granted to reign upon His throne the King of Ethiopia, Solomon's firstborn.

65. MARY THE DAUGHTER OF DAVID

Joseph was the son of David and Mary was also the daughter of David. Therefore was Mary promised in marriage to Joseph her kinsman, as it is said in the gospel: "O Joseph, son of David, fear thou not to take to wife Mary thy bride, for that which is to be born of her is of the Holy Spirit, the Word of God."[1]

And there was born of her, God the Word, Light of Light, Son of the Father, Who came and delivered His creation from the hand of Satan and from Sheol: and from death He hath delivered all of us who have believed in Him; He hath drawn us to His father and hath raised us up into heaven His throne, to become His heirs; for He is a lover of mankind, and unto Him praise belongeth forever.

66. THE KING OF ROME

The kingdom of Rome was the portion and dominion of Japhet, the son of Noah. They planned and they made twelve great cities, and Darius built the greatest cities of their kingdom: Antioch, Tyre, Parthia and Rome, and those who reigned dwelt there; and King Constantine built Constantinople after his own name... the sign of the Cross having appeared to him during the battle in the form of stars cut in heaven, he was delivered out of the hands of his enemy; and from that time onwards the Kings of Rome made their habitation there.

Darius had many descendants; and from Darius to the days of Solomon were eighteen generations. And of his seed was born a man whose name was Zanbares, who in his wisdom, made a drawing of the astrolabe,[2] and placed stars therein, and a balance for the sun. And he visioned what would happen in those days; that the kingdom would not remain to the children of Japhet but would depart to the seed of David, of the tribe of Shem. And when he thus saw, he sent a message to David the King, saying: "Take my daughter for thy son." *And David the King took her, and gave her to Solomon his son, and Solomon begot a son by her and called his name Adramis.*

---

[1]Matthew 1:20

[2]Instrument for observing the positions of the celestial body now superseded by the sextant.

Zanbares died before this and Baltasor, who was of his kinsmen, became king. He lacked male offspring to reign after him upon his throne, and he was jealous lest the children of his father should reign after him. And he sent a written message to Solomon the King, saying, "Hail to the greatness of thy kingdom, and to thy honourable wisdom! Do give me thy son whom I will make king over the city of Rome. For I have not been able to father male children, but only three daughters. I will give him whichever of my daughters he pleaseth, and I will give him my throne, and he shall be king, he and his seed after him in the city of Rome forever."

When King Solomon had read this letter, he meditated, saying: "If I keep back my son he will send to the King of the East, who will give him his son, and that which I have planned will be made void; therefore I will give him my son." And he took counsel with his counsellors of the house of Israel, and he said unto them: "We have already given our son and our children to the country of Ethiopia, and Israel hath a kingdom there. And now, so that we may have a third kingdom, the country of Rome, I will send Adramis, my youngest son.

Hold it not against me as an evil thing, that formerly I took away your sons, for it is a pleasing thing to God that the men of Ethiopia have learned His Name, and have become His people. In like manner the men of Rome, if we give them our children will become the people of God. The people of Israel have taken the kingdom of Ethiopia and the kingdom of Rome. Give ye your youngest sons as before ye gave the eldest and let those of middle age stay in our city."

Then the men of Israel rose up and took counsel, and returned, and said unto him: "We will speak this matter unto the King, and he shall do his will." And he said unto them: "Make me hear what ye would say." And they said unto him: "Thou hast already taken the eldest son from our houses, and now take the youngest of the children." And he was pleased with this counsel, and he did for them as they wished.

And he brought forward his son Adramis, who did take some of the nobles of the lower grades of the house of Israel, and they gave him a priest of the tribe of the Levites whose name was Akimihel, and they set Adramis upon the king's mule, and cried out to him: "Hail! Long live the royal father!" And all the people said: "It is right and proper."

And they anointed him with the holy oil of kingship, and commanded him to keep all the laws of the kingdom, and they made him to swear that he would worship no other god except the God of Israel. And they blessed him as they had blessed David his brother, and admonished Adramis even as they had admonished David, and they accompanied him on his way as far as the sea coast.

And Solomon the King wrote and sent a letter saying: "Peace be to Baltasor, the King of Rome! Take my son Adramis, and give him thy daughter and make him king in the city of Rome. Thou didst wish for a king of the seed of David my father, and I have done thy will. Also I have sent unto thee his nobles, fourteen on his right hand and fourteen on his left, who shall keep the Law with him and be subject unto thee according to thy will." And they arrived there with the ambassadors of the King of Rome, together with much splendour and all the equipment that was required for the country of Rome.

And they came to the city of Rome, to Baltasor the King, and they repeated all that Solomon had sent them to say, and delivered over to him his son. And Baltasor rejoiced exceedingly, and gave him his eldest daughter, whose name was Adlonya; and he made a great marriage feast according to the greatness of his kingdom, and established him over all his city of Rome. And he blessed him, for he was noble in stature, and his wisdom was marvellous, and he was exceedingly mighty in his strength.

One day Baltasor wished to test his knowledge in the trying of cases. A man, the owner of a vineyard, came to him and appealed to him, saying: "My Lord, Arsani, the son of Yodad, hath laid waste my vineyard with his sheep. And behold, I have seized his sheep and they are in my house; what decision wilt thou come to in respect of me?" And the owner of the sheep came to the King and made an appeal to him, saying: "Give me back my sheep, for he hath carried them off because they went into his vineyard." And the King said unto them: "Go ye and argue your case before your King Adramis, and whatsoever he shall say unto you, that do." And they came and argued their case before him.

Then Adramis asked him, saying: "How much of the vineyard have the sheep eaten? The leaves, or the tendrils or the young grapes, or the shoots by the roots?" And the owner of the vineyard answered and said unto him: "They have eaten the tendrils and the branches that had grapes upon them, and there is nothing left of the vines except the twigs by the roots." Adramis then asked the owner of the sheep: "Is this true?" And the owner of the sheep answered and said unto him: "My lord, they ate only the tendrils with leaves on them."

Adramis then answered and said: "This man saith that they ate the grapes; is this true?" And the owner of the sheep answered and said: "No my lord, but they ate the blossoms before they had formed into grapes."

67. THE FIRST JUDGMENT OF ADRAMIS, KING OF ROME

Adramis then said unto them: "Hearken ye to the judgment which I will declare unto you. If the sheep have destroyed all the shoots from the root of the vine, then they all belong to thee. And if they have eaten the leaves of the branches, and the blossoms of the grapes, take the sheep, shear their wool, and take also the young sheep which have not yet brought forth young ones. But the sheep which have already brought forth young ones for the first time, leave to the owner of the sheep."

All those who heard the judgment which he pronounced, marvelled, and Baltasor said: "Verily, this judgment is a judgment of the people of the God of Israel. Henceforth judge him that hath a case at law, wage war with him that would wage war, rule him that would be ruled, keep alive him that should be kept alive, and pass the judgment that ought to be passed according as men would be judged, and take this city to thyself and to thy seed after thee."

And all the men of the city of Rome were well pleased, and they made Adramis king over them, and they rejoiced in him with a great joy; for it happened thus by the Will of God.

After this, a fever seized Baltasor, and he sent Adramis to the war, and into everything that he wished, whilst he himself remained in the city; after this Baltasor died, and Adramis directed the kingdom. And the city of Rome became the possession of Adramis and of his generations after him, *for by the Will of God the kingdoms of the world were given to the seed of Shem, and slavery to the seed of Ham, and the handicraft is of the seed to Japhet.*[1]

68. THE KING OF MEDYAM

The king of Medyam was of the seed of Shem. For of the seed of Isaac was Esau, who went forth from his mother's womb with Jacob clinging to the sole of his foot; and Jacob carried away the right of the firstborn from Esau for the sake of a bowl of porridge.

And the name of Esau's kingdom was called, according to his name of contempt, "Edom", for the meaning of Edom is "lentils;" and because of this the seed of Esau were called "Edomites." For through the greed of his belly he forsook and lost the right of the firstborn of the seed of Shem.

And unless the soul be restrained by temperance, it will bring down into a net the whole lust of the belly which is of the body. For the body is greedy, but temperance restraineth the soul, and therefore Paul said: "That which the soul doth not wish the body wisheth; and that which the body doth not wish the soul wisheth, and so each contends against the other."[2] I If a man willeth a thing and his soul joined itself with his desire he becometh like Christ.

The Apostles say that Christ is the Head of every man who travelleth upon the straight road. And our Lord said unto His disciples: "Walk in the Spirit and perform ye not the lusts of your bodies." And when they heard this they forsook all the lust of the flesh, and they said unto our Lord: "Behold now, we have forsaken everything and followed Thee; what is our reward?" And our Saviour said unto them: "Ye have made your bodies like unto those of the angels, and ye shall do mighty deeds even as I do. And behold, I have given you authority to raise the dead, and I have given you power to heal the sick and ye shall trample upon all the power of the enemy. And at My second coming ye shall judge and put to shame the Twelve Tribes of Israel, because they have not

---

[1]Genesis 9:18-17   [2]Galatians 5:17

believed on Me, and have treated My glory with contempt. As for those who believe in Me, ye shall magnify them and shall make them to rejoice with you in My kingdom."

69. THE KING OF BABYLON

It came to pass in days of old that there lived in the kingdom of Manasseh, King of Israel, a certain man whose name was Karmin, and he was a fearer of God, and he gave many alms and offerings to the poor of Israel. And when he made offerings to the House of God, he did so with sincerity, and his tithe he gave double; and he was good in all his ways, and there was no evil whatsoever before him. But Satan, the enemy of all good, became envious of him, for he saw that his course in life was good.

And that man Karmin was exceedingly rich in camels, horses, flocks of sheep, herds of cattle, gold and silver and fine apparel, and he used to feed the mule of the king in Armatem, a city of Israel. His native place was the country of Judah, his father's portion, but because of his love for wealth, he departed into Armatem to dwell there, and Israel allowed him to settle there because of his riches; for he was exceedingly rich and had many possessions, and the governors of Judah were afraid of him.

70. CONCERNING LYING WITNESSES

And there was a certain depraved man of the seed of Benjamin, whose name was Benyas, who used to lead the mule of the King of Israel, and Karmin used to feed him, together with the mule of King Manasseh. And among the neighbours of Karmin there were certain men who were envious of him because of his pastures and wells, and because of the multitude of his flocks and herds and servants... for the region where he had settled was the inheritance of their fathers, and for this reason they wished to drive him away from their country.

So they kept watch upon Benyas, the leader of the King's mule, with evil intent, and they slandered and abused Karmin, and said unto Benyas: "This Karmin hath blasphemed the King of Israel, the anointed of God, saying: 'This king is not the son of a free woman, but the son of an old woman servant who was bought for two measures of grain to work at mill and brickmaking.' Do thou take this case against him to the king and accuse him, for we will be thy witnesses before the king, and we will not let thee be put to shame." And they made a covenant together, and they swore to him that they would bear false witness against Karmin, by whose tongue such words were never uttered, and into whose mind such thoughts had never entered.

So Benyas went to his Lord, the King, and told him all this matter. And the King said unto him: "Is there any man who hath heard this with thee?" And Benyas answered and said unto him: "Yes my Lord, there are some who have heard... two of the nobles of Israel who belong to Armatem." And the King said unto him: "Go now and bring them here secretly so that we may find out whether they agree with thy words; and if they do, we will cut off the head of Karmin."

Benyas then departed and brought Zaryos and Karmelos, of the tribe of Manasseh... for it had been agreed between them that they would not put him to shame before the King, in the matter of their lying testimony.

And these two men agreed together and planned when they were on their way, saying: "When we have spoken to the King, if he shall ask us afterwards separately so that he may find out the truth of our words: 'Where did you hear these words?' we will each of us answer and say: 'When we were drinking wine with him.' And when he shall say to us: 'What day was this?' we will say: 'Five days after the new moon.' And when he saith unto us: 'What time of the day?' we will say unto him: 'At the ninth hour, where he was sitting with us, and we were drinking wine together.' And when he shall ask us saying: 'What did ye drink out of and where were you sitting?' we will say unto him: 'Out of cups of gold, and our seats were in the hall of his house where the cushions were placed'."

And they agreed together on this evil plot while they were on the way to the King.

When they arrived in the presence of the King, Benyas brought them forward, and the King questioned them... and they repeated to him all their lying counsel. And he asked them as they had surmised on the road… the occasion, the day and the hour of their drinking, and their sitting in the hall and they told him.

And when the King had enquired into all this matter, and dismissed them, he called the captain of his host who stood before him, and said unto him: "Go at dawn of day tomorrow and surround the house of Karmin and let not any of his people escape thee, neither man nor woman, and slay them all with the sword. As for Karmin, cut of this head, and bring hither all his possessions, his goods, all his flocks and herds and his gold and silver."

And those liars rejoiced and returned to their district, and they went in to the house of Karmin and held converse with him with words of peace, and they paid him compliments, and they spoke kindly before his face, evil being in their hearts. Then was fulfilled on them the prophecy of David, who said: "Those who speak words of peace with their neighbour and have evil in their hearts, reward them according to the evil of their works and according to the evil of their thoughts."[1]

And they drank themselves drunk in the house of Karmin, and they fell asleep there with him; but when they had fallen asleep, behold, the Angel of God was sent to Karmin, and he awoke him and said unto him: "Leave all thy possessions and save thyself, for soldiers have been commanded by Manasseh the King to cut off thy head. Take as much of thy riches as thou canst carry, and flee into another country, for this Manasseh is a slayer of the prophets and a seeker after the blood of innocent men."

Then Karmin rose up immediately and sought out his treasure in gold and took it, and he awoke his wife and his two sons, also his chosen servants, and loaded them with possessions of great value, and went forth by night.

He sent off his wife and his sons with two servants to Jerusalem, and he himself departed with two of his servants to a remote country, a distance of three months journey; and he arrived in Babylon. And so he came to

---

[1] Psalm 28:3,4

Balaon the King of Babylon, and gave him gifts, and related unto him what had happened to him. And Balaon sympathized with Karmin, and gave him a habitation near the house of his merchant, who had departed to a far country for a period of three years.

And those men, Zaryos and Karmelos, who had made lying testimony against Karmin, were killed drunk in bed in Karmin's house.

****

And the wife of the merchant loved Karmin, and she was seduced by him, and became with child. The husband of the woman had left on his journey when she was with child, and she delivered and gave the child to a nurse who brought it up. Then, in the second year she went astray and became pregnant with child by Karmin, for the person of Karmin was exceedingly good in Israel. And the woman wished to throw the child whom she had conceived into the river when he was born and to wait for her husband, the merchant, as if she had not gone astray, and had not done anything wrong, even as the wicked woman, who, having wronged her husband and washed herself, sitteth down like a woman who hath done nothing, and she sweareth an oath falsely.

And at that time the wife of Balaon, the King of Babylon, also conceived and brought forth something which was like an eagle... like a bird, but altogether without wings. And she called a handmaiden who was a favourite, and sent the thing away in a wicker-basket and commanded her to cast it into the river, without letting anyone know about it.

And the time came for the wife of the merchant to give birth, and she brought forth a man-child, comely in form and worthy of compassion. And without suckling it she called to her favourite handmaiden, and put it into a box and commanded her to throw him into the river without anyone knowing about it, for she was afraid of her husband.

That same night two women were delivered of child, the merchant's wife and the wife of the King, and at daybreak the two women sent their handmaidens to cast their children into the river.

By the Will of God these two handmaidens met each other before they had thrown the children into the river, and they talked, and the handmaiden of the Queen asked the handmaiden of the merchant, saying: "What is in thy box?" And she showed her the beautiful child. And she further said unto her: "Why hast thou brought him here?" And the merchant's handmaiden said unto her: "Because the wife of my lord hath gone astray with a certain Israelite, and she conceived and brought forth this child, and she hath commanded me to throw him into the river." And the Queen's handmaiden said unto her: "Why does she not bring up a child who is so beautiful?" and the merchant's handmaiden said unto her: "Her husband left her with child and she brought forth a child, and is rearing him; how then can she rear this other child who is of a strange and alien seed?"

Then the merchant's handmaiden asked the Queen's handmaiden, saying: "What hast thou in thy basket?" And the Queen's handmaiden said unto her: "My lady brought forth a child that hath not the appearance of a man but that of a wingless eagle, and she hath commanded me to throw it into the river. So now, give me this child of thine that I may give it to my mistress, and do thou take this bird and cast it into the river." And they did so.

And the handmaiden of the Queen took the child of Karmin to her mistress, and the Queen rejoiced, and it was reported to the King that the Queen had borne a son. And the Queen gave the boy to the nurses, and he grew up in the palace of the King, and she called his name Nebuchadnezzar... which being interpreted means, "Saved by the feather of a bird."

So then, the King of Babylon is of the seed of Shem, and he came and overthrew Jerusalem by the Will of God, and he carried away captive the Children of Israel... and he made them to wander in Babylon with the grandchildren of Manasseh.

The King of Babylon was so very rich that he set up a pillar of gold on the plain of Babylon sixty cubits high, and he was very arrogant, and he used to say: "I make the sun to shine in the heavens;" and he worshipped idols. But God abased and humbled him so that he might know Him, and He set his portion with the beasts of the field. And when he knew the name of the Lord, after seven years, He had compassion upon him, and brought him back in repentance. And the kingdom of Babylon[1] was his, and it belonged to those who were of his seed forever.

71. THE KING OF PERSIA

The King of Persia is likewise of the seed of Shem. Judah had two sons, and he had given Tamar to his eldest son, but he died. Judah then sent his younger son to her, that he might bring forth seed and inheritors to his brother by his brother's wife, but he did that which God hated, for he did not wish to raise up seed to his brother as his father Judah had commanded him; so when he lay with Tamar he made his seed to go upon the ground, so that it might not germinate in her womb and be called the seed of his brother. Rather, he wished to raise up children by his own wife in his own name. And when God saw his evil act He turned His face away from him and slew him.

Then Judah, the father-in-law of Tamar, brought her back and set her in the house of her father, and said unto her people: "Keep carefully this Israelite woman, and let her not defile herself with an alien... for I have a small son, and if God will let him grow up, I will give him to her."

One day, while Tamar was living as a widow in her father's house, behold Judah, her father-in-law came to the place where his sheep were. And when Tamar heard that her father-in-law had come there, she cast away from her the apparel of widowhood and dressed herself in splendid garments, and she veiled herself after the manner of an harlot...and she followed him and sat down.

Judah then sent a message to her, saying: "I wish to be with thee." And she said unto him: "What wilt thou give me for my hire?" And he said unto her: "I will send to thee in the morning early, a lamb." She then said unto him: "Give me a token until thou givest me the lamb." Judah then gave her his staff, his ring, and the close-fitting cap that was under his outer garment.

---

[1]Modern-day Iraq

After he had slept with her, she took the things and departed unto her house. When he sent the lamb unto her early in the morning, and his servants enquired saying: "Where is the house of the harlot?" It was said unto them: "There is no harlot in our town." So they returned into their city and told him that there was no harlot in that town. And Judah said: "Leave it… the Will of God be done."

When Tamar conceived and they told her father-in-law this, he went and took the elders of Israel to the father of Tamar, and said unto him: "Bring to me thy daughter Tamar who hath conceived, that we may stone her with stones even as Moses commanded, for she hath brought reproach upon the house of Israel."

When it was reported to Tamar, that her father-in-law spoke thus, she brought out the staff, the ring and the cap, and gave them to her father, and said unto the elders of Israel: "The owner of these things hath seduced me; let them stone me with him… with stones."

When Judah saw his possessions he recognized them, and he said: "Tamar is more righteous than I."[1] Then he left and came to his house. And Tamar brought forth twins, two nations… Perez and Zara. Persia[2] was founded in the name of Perez, and he ruled over it and his seed after him, and they were called Persians. Behold, it is proved that the King of Persia is of the seed of Shem.

72. CONCERNING THE KING OF MOAB

The King of Moab is also of the seed of Shem, for when God made Abraham to depart from his father's country into the land of Harran, He made Lot to pass over into the land of Sodom and Gomorrah, then He sent His Angels, Michael and Gabriel, to bring out Lot and to burn up the cities of Sodom and Gomorrah; and they destroyed them and brought out Lot with his children.

The wrath of God had come down on the city of Sodom as a rain of fire from heaven, which burned up mountains and hills, stones and earth,

---

[1]Genesis 38:13-26   [2]Modern-day Iran

and lightnings and peals of thunder came down mingled with the crashing sound of the wrath of God, and a cloud of fire made the heat to emit smoke.

When all this uproar was being heard, the Angels said unto Lot: "Turn not around after ye have gone forth from the city, turn not round that ye die not." But when Akmaba the wife of Lot heard this she did turn around so that she might see the city of her father and her mother, and she became a pillar of salt... and she remaineth thus to this day, to this very day.

As for Lot, God made him to dwell in the mountains of Ararat, and there he planted a new vineyard, but his daughters made their father to drink wine, and they plotted a wicked plot, and they said: "Why shall the possession of our father be wasted? Our mother has been destroyed on the road, and there is no one here to marry us." And they made their father drunk, and his elder daughter lay with him whilst his mind was clouded with wine, and Lot the righteous man did not know when his daughter lay with him and when she rose up from him, for his mind was clouded with strong drink, therefore the act of lying with his daughter was not reckoned against Lot as sin, for he did it unknowingly.

And his elder daughter brought forth a child, and she called him "Moab," which being interpreted means, "From my father, on my knee." Moab then was the father of the Moabites and the Agarenes. Behold now, it is clear that the King of Moab is of the seed of Shem.[1]

73. THE KING OF AMALEK, A DESCENDANT OF LOT

And it came to pass that when the elder daughter of Lot had brought forth her son, she said unto the younger daughter: "Come, let us make our father drink wine, so that thou also may company with him and get offspring." Again they prepared wine, and they spoke to him the words of deceit, and said, unto him: "Drink wine, O father... so that thy heart may be comforted." And he, the simple man, drank and became drunk, and again when he had drunk and his mind was clouded with wine, the

---

[1]Genesis 19:30-38

younger daughter came and lay with him, and he did not know of her Living with him, or her rising up from him. And she also conceived and gave birth to a son, and she called him, "Ammon", and he is the father of the Amalekites. Behold now, it is clear that the King of Amalek is also of the seed of Shem.·[1]

74. THE KING OF THE PHILISTINES

And behold, how the seed of Samson reigned over the Philistines. Samson was of the seed of Dan, one of the twelve sons of Jacob, and he was the son of a handmaiden of Jacob.

The Angel of the Lord had appeared to the mother of Samson and said unto her: "Keep thyself from all pollution and company with no other man except thy husband... for he who shall be borne of thee shall be a Nazarite, holy to the Lord, and he shall be the deliverer of Israel from the hand of the Philistines."[2] And then she brought forth Samson.

And again the Angel appeared unto her and said unto her: "Thou shalt not let a razor go upon his head, and he shall neither eat flesh nor drink wine, and he shall marry no strange woman but only a woman of his own people, and from the house of his father."[3] And how God gave him strength ye have heard from the Book of Judges.[4] But Samson transgressed the commandment of God and married a daughter of the uncircumcised Philistines.

Because of this God was wroth, and He delivered him into the hands of men of the uncircumcised Philistines, and they blinded his eyes, and they made him act as a clown in the house of their king.

When Samson pulled the roof down upon them, he had killed seven hundred thousand of them with the iron, with the stone and with his staff, and with the jaw of an ass. For their number was as that of the locusts, until he released Israel from the service of the Philistines.

****

---

[1]Genesis 19:30-38   [2]Judges 13: 2-5
[3]Judges 13:9-14   [4]Judges 15, 16

Delilah had conceived by Samson, and whilst she was with child Samson died with the Philistines, and Delilah brought forth a son and she called his name "Menahem", which means being interpreted, "Seed of the strong man."

Delilah was the sister of Maksaba, the wife of the King of the Philistines, and Samson slew the King of the Philistines in his palace with his people and his household, and died with him. Then Delilah went to her sister Maksaba, the Queen of the Philistines.

Both women were beautiful and they had no children, but both had conceived... and the husbands of both were dead. The two women loved each other exceedingly, with their love for each other not as the love of sisters, but that of the mother for the child, and of the child for the mother; even so was their love.

The rulership over those who were left of the slaughter made by Samson in the palace of the King was in the hands of Maksaba, for none of the mighty men of war of the kingdom of the Philistines were left, and therefore Maksaba ruled over those that were left.

And they spoke to her morning and evening, saying: "We have no other king except thyself, and except that one that shall go forth from thy belly. If our god Dagon will do a favour unto us, that which is in thy belly shall be a son, who shall reverence our god Dagon and shall reign over us. And if it be a daughter we will make her to reign over us, so that thy name and the name of Kwolason our lord, shall be your memorial over us."

Maksaba brought forth a man-child and all the men of the Philistines rejoiced, and they did homage to her and sang, saying: "Dagon and Bel have honoured and loved Maksaba, and the seed of Kwolason is again with us."

Delilah also bore a son, and the two women brought up the children in great state and dignity; and when the children were five years old they ate and played together before them, and the mothers made garments of costly material for them, and set daggers above their loins, and chains of gold on their necks. And the people seated the son of Maksaba on the throne of his father, and made him king over the Philistines.

75. HOW THE SON OF SAMSON SLEW THE SON OF THE KING OF THE PHILISTINES

Akamhel, the son of Samson, spoke unto his mother Delilah, saying: "Why am I not reigning and sitting upon this throne?" And his mother said unto him: "Cease my son. This throne did not belong to thy father, and this city was not thy father's city; when the God of thy father let thee grow up thou shalt go to thy father's throne." And her son said unto her: "I will neither forsake thee my mother, nor Maksaba my aunt, and I will be king here."

One day the two youths were drunk after their meal was ended, and the doors were shut. The two women were sitting together about to eat flesh; the two youths were playing before them, and they ate with them, and a maidservant held the dish between them. Then Akamhel, the son of Delilah, took from the dish a piece of flesh which would fill both his hands, and put it to his mouth, and Tebreles the son of Maksaba, the Queen of the Philistines, snatched away that part of the flesh that was outside his mouth. And Akamhel drew his sword and cut of this head, and it fell into the dish before he could swallow what he had seized; and his body fell upon the pavement of the house, and his hands and feet twitched convulsively, and he died.

Fear and dismay laid hold upon their two mothers, and they spoke not a word to anyone because they were afraid, but they swallowed the food which was in their mouths, and they looked at each other, not knowing what to do.

Then a handmaiden rose up and took the head of Tebreles out of the dish, and put it back on its neck and covered it with her garment... And Delilah rose up and seized the sword of the dead son of her sister, and went to kill her own son Akamhel, but he saved himself by hiding behind a pillar.

Then her sister rose up and seized her, saying: "Why should we be destroyed through their quarrel? This youth is spring of a bad root and cannot bear good fruit; come my sister, let him not destroy thee also."

So she took the sword from her hand, and fetched rich purple clothing which kings wear, and she gave it to him, and she spoke kind words unto him, saying: "Take the apparel, my son, and thou thyself sit upon the throne of their kingdom of the Philistines."

Akamhel raged like a savage bear, for he wanted to slay both women until they decided to leave the house… and they went out, and when he had made them to leave the house he took the purple apparel, and went out. The women then came back and made the dead body ready for burial, and they buried it secretly.

When the time for the evening meal had come, the young men and their maidservants searched for their king and found him not, and they asked about him, and his mother said unto them: "Your king is sick, and this man will sit in place of him." And they took him and set him on the throne, and they prepared a feast and rejoiced.

And from that time onward the son of Samson reigned over them, and there was none who transgressed his orders. He had committed this act of murder fifteen winters after he was born, and the kingdom of the Philistines became his and his seed's after him. So then, it is proven that the kingdom of the Philistines belongeth to the seed of Shem.

76. ABRAHAM'S JOURNEY INTO EGYPT

When God had given unto Abraham glory and riches, he lacked a son. And Sarah and Abraham talked together on their bed, and he said unto her: "Thou art barren." And she said unto him: "It is not I who am barren but thyself." And they continued to discuss the matter and to dispute about it.

And there came a famine in the land of Canaan, and Abraham heard that there was food in the land of Egypt, the country of Pharaoh. So, as Abraham had spent all his possessions in charity to the poor during the days of the famine, and not having provided for the morrow, when the famine waxed strong in the land of Canaan, he lacked food to eat. And he said: "I give thanks unto God that what he hath given unto me I have expended on my servants. But as for thee Sarah, come, let us go into the land of Egypt in order to save ourselves from death by famine. "And she said unto him: "Thy will be done O my Lord, and if thou die I will die with thee, and if thou live I will live with thee; it is not for me to oppose thy word." And they rose up and set out on the journey to Egypt.

When they drew nigh to Egypt, Abraham said unto Sarah: "One thing I must ask of thee; and Sarah said: "Speak, my Lord." And he said unto her: "I have heard that the habits of the Egyptians are lawless, and that they live in idolatry and fornication. So, when they have seen thee they will plot evil against me, and slay me because of the charm of thy beautiful form; for there is among them no one that can be compared unto thee.

And now, in order to save my life, do say, if they happen to ask thee questions about me, 'I am his sister,' so that my soul be saved from death by the hand of the strangers." And Sarah said: "Thy will be done. The word which thou tellest me I will speak, and what thou asketh of me I will do." And they wept and worshipped God, and they came into the great city of the King of Egypt.

When the Egyptians saw Abraham and Sarah they marvelled at the beauty of their appearance, for they imagined that they had been brought forth by the same mother. And they said unto Abraham: "What is this woman to thee?" And Abraham said unto them: "She is my sister." Therefore the people made a report to Pharaoh that a couple of lovely form had arrived, one a woman and the other a young man, and that there was no one beautiful like unto them in all the land.

Pharaoh rejoiced, and he sent a message to Abraham, saying: "Give me thy sister that I may marry her to myself." And Abraham pondered in his mind, saying: "If I keep her back he will kill me and take her;" so he said: "Do so, provided that thou make me well comfortable." Pharaoh then gave him one thousand silver pieces and took Sarah to make her his wife; and he brought her into his palace, and set her upon his bed and Pharaoh the King of Egypt prepared to company with her.

But behold the Angel of the Lord appeared unto him by night carrying a sword of fire, and he drew close to him, and he lighted up the whole chamber with his fiery flame, and he wanted to slay Pharaoh.

Pharaoh fled from one wall of the chamber to the other, and from one corner of the chamber to the other; wherever he went the Angel followed him. Then Pharaoh stretched out his hands and said unto the Angel: "O Lord, forgive me this my sin." And the Angel said unto him: "Why dost thou attack the wife of another man?" And Pharaoh said unto him: "O Lord, slay thou not innocent blood, for he said unto me 'She is my sister,' and therefore I took her to myself innocently. What shall I do to deliver myself from thy hands?" And the Angel said unto him: "Give Abraham's wife back to him, and give him a gift, and send him away to his own country."

Then Pharaoh called Abraham and gave unto him his wife Sarah, together with a handmaiden whose name was Hagar, and he gave unto him gold and silver, and costly garments, and sent him away in peace.[1]

So, Abraham and his wife returned to their country in peace. And Sarah said unto Abraham: "I know that I am barren. Take thou the handmaiden whom Pharaoh gave unto me; it may be that God will give thee seed in her. As for me, my person is old and withered, and the flower of my body hath dried up."

And she gave Hagar unto him. And Abraham took Hagar and she conceived by him, and she brought forth a son and called his name Ishmael, which means, "God hath heard me."[2]

Afterwards God gave Abraham seed from his wife Sarah and he fathered Isaac, but Sarah became jealous of Ishmael the son of the handmaiden, because he would reach manhood before her son, and she said in her heart: "It may be that he will slay my son and inherit his father's house."

Abraham then offered up offerings to God and said: "Lord, what shall I do in respect of Ishmael my son, my firstborn? I wish that he may live for me before Thee, but Sarah my wife is jealous because Thou hast given me seed in her old age." Ishmael was fourteen years old before Isaac was born.

---

[1]Genesis 12:14-20   [2]Genesis 16:3-16

And God said unto Abraham: "What Sarah said is true; cast out the handmaiden with her son Ishmael. Let Ishmael live before Me, and I will make him a great nation, and he shall father twelve nations and shall reign over them; but I will establish My covenant with Isaac My servant, the son of Sarah, and in him I will bless all the nations of the earth, and in the heavens also I will make him king."[1]

For as God swore, He gave all the kingdoms of the world to the seed of Shem, also an exalted throne and dominion, even as his father Noah, by the word of God, blessed his son Shem, saying: "Be lord to thy brethren and reign over them." *And this that he said had reference to the Redeemer, the King of us all, Jesus Christ the King of heaven and earth, Who magnified kings, and who when He pleaseth brings down their power; for unto Him belong power and dominion over all created things for ever and ever.*

77. THE KING OF ETHIOPIA RETURNS TO HIS COUNTRY

And the King of Ethiopia returned to his country with joy and gladness; and marching along with their songs, their pipes and their chariots, like an army of heavenly beings, the Ethiopians arrived from Jerusalem at the city of Wakerom in a single day... and they sent messengers to announce their arrival to Makeda the Queen of Ethiopia, and to report to her how they had found every good thing, and how her son had become King, and how they had brought the heavenly Zion.

And she caused all this glorious news to be spread abroad, and she made a herald to go round about in all the country that was her dominion, ordering the people to meet her son, and especially the heavenly Zion, the Tabernacle of the God of Israel. And they blew horns before her, and all the people of Ethiopia rejoiced, from the least to the greatest... and the soldiers rose up with her to meet their King.

And she came to the city of the government, which is the chief city of the kingdom of Ethiopia; which in later times became the chief city of the Christians of Ethiopia... and in it she caused to be prepared numerous

---

[1]Genesis 12

perfumes from India, to be used there. And her son came by the Azyaba road to Wakerom, then came forth to Masas, ascended to Bur and arrived at the city of the government, the capital city of Ethiopia, which the Queen herself had built and called "Dabra Makeda", after her own name.

David II the King came with great pomp unto his mother's city, and then it was that she saw in the heights the heavenly Zion sending forth light like the sun. And when the Queen saw this, she gave thanks unto the God of Israel, and praised Him. And she bowed low and reverenced Zion, and threw up her head and gazed into the heavens and thanked her Creator... then she clapped her hands together and sent forth shouts of laughter from her mouth, and danced on the ground with her feet; and she adorned her whole body with joy and gladness.

Pavillions and tents were placed at the foot of Dabra Makeda on the flat plain by the side of good waters... and they slaughtered thirty-two thousand stalled oxen and bulls. And they set Zion upon the fortress of Dabra Makeda, and made ready for her three hundred guards who wielded swords to watch over the Tabernacle of Zion, together with her own men and her nobles, the mighty men of Israel. And her own guards were three hundred men who bore swords, and in addition to these her son David had seven hundred guards.

They rejoiced exceedingly with great glory and pleasure and they were arrayed in fine and costly apparel, for the kingdom was directed by her... from the Sea of Aleba to the Sea of Oseka, and everyone obeyed her command.

Queen Makeda had such great honour and riches, that none before her ever had the like, and none after her shall ever have the like. In those days Solomon was King in Jerusalem, and Makeda was Queen in Ethiopia. Unto both of them were given wisdom, glory, riches, graciousness and understanding, and beauty of voice, eloquence of speech and intelligence. Gold and silver were held as cheaply as brass, and rich fabrics wherein gold was woven were as common as linen garments... and the cattle and the horses were innumerable.

78. HOW QUEEN MAKEDA MADE HER SON KING OF ETHIOPIA

On the third day of the celebrations Makeda delivered over to her son seventeen thousand chosen horses, which were to watch the army of the enemy, and one thousand chosen mules, apparel of honour, gold and silver measured by the omer:[1] and she delivered over to her son everything that was his by law, and the throne of her kingdom.

And the Queen said unto her nobles: "Speak ye now, and swear by the heavenly Zion that ye will not make women queens or set them upon the throne of the kingdom of Ethiopia, and that no one except the male seed of David, the son of Solomon the King, shall ever reign over Ethiopia, and that ye will never make women queens." And all the nobles of the king's house swore, also the governors, the councillors and the administrators.

And she made Almeyas and Azariah the chief of the priests and the chief of the deacons, and the sons of the mighty men of Israel performed the Law, together with their King David in the Tabernacle of Witness... *and the kingdom was made anew.*

Then the hearts of the people shone at the sight of Zion, the Tabernacle of the Law of God... and the people of Ethiopia cast aside their idols, and they worshipped their Creator, the God Who had made them. And the men of Ethiopia loved the righteousness and justice that God loveth.

They forsook their former fornications and chose purity in the camp that was in the sight of the heavenly Zion. They forsook the pleasure of the gods who were devils, and chose the service and praise of God.

The daughters of Jerusalem suffered disgrace, and the daughters of Ethiopia were held in honour; the daughter of Judah was sad, but the daughter of Ethiopia rejoiced.

The people of Ethiopia were chosen from among idols and graven images, and the people of Israel were rejected. The daughters of Zion were rejected, and the daughters of Ethiopia were honoured... for God

---

[1]Hebrew measure; about half a gallon dry measure.

accepted the peoples who had been cast away, and rejected Israel, *for Zion was taken away from them and she came into the country of Ethiopia... for wherever God is pleased for her to dwell, there is her habitation.*

And Makeda, the Queen of Ethiopia, gave the kingdom to her son David II, the son of Solomon, the King of Israel, and she said unto him: "Take the kingdom, I have given it unto thee. I have made King him whom God hath made King, and I have chosen him whom God hath chosen as the keeper of His Tabernacle".

Then the king rose up and girded his apparel, and he bowed low before his mother, and said unto her: "Thou art the Queen, O my Lady, and I will serve thee in everything which thou commandest me, whether it be to death or whether it be to life. Wheresoever thou sendest me I will go, and whatsoever thou commandest me to do, that I will do. For thou art the head and I am the foot, and thou art the Queen and I am thy slave; everything shall be performed according to thy order and none shall transgress thy commandment.

And behold, we have brought with us the whole Law of the kingdom and the commandment of God, which Zadok the High Priest declared unto us when he anointed me with the oil of sovereignty in the house of the sanctuary of God... the horn of oil, which is the unguent of priesthood and royalty, being in his hand. And he did unto us that which was written in the Law... and we were anointed... Azariah to the priesthood and I to the kingdom; then Almeyas, the mouth of God and keeper of the Law and of Zion... the ear of the King in every path of righteousness.

They also told us and made us to understand that we bear death and life, and that we are like a man who hath fire in his left hand and water in his right, and who can put his hand into whichever he pleaseth. For punishment and life are written therein.

And so, Almeyas and Azariah brought forth that writing which was written before God and before the King of Israel, and they read it before Makeda and before the great men of Israel. And when they heard these words, all those who were round about bowed down and made obeisance, and they glorified God, He who had made them hear these words and had given them this commandment, so that they might perform the justice and judgment of God.

The Queen then said unto her son: "My son, God hath given unto thee righteousness... walk thou therein and withdraw not thyself from if for ye are the guardians of the Law of God and the guides of His commandments... ye are the men of the House of God and the guardians of Zion, the Tabernacle of the Law of God."

79. WHAT YE SHALL EAT: THE CLEAN AND THE UNCLEAN

This is what ye shall eat: the ox, the sheep, the goat, the buffalo and the antelope, the gazelle, and every creature with a cleft hoof eat ye, and also the creatures that chew the cud. But ye shall not eat the camel, the rabbit and the coney, for they chew the cud but their hoofs are not cleft. The wolf and the pig ye shall not eat, for their hoofs are clean but they do not chew the cud... Ye shall not eat what is unclean.

Whatsoever is in the waters with fins and scales, eat ye; but whatsoever is unclean therein, eat ye not. Among birds everything that is clean eat ye, but ye shall not eat the following: the eagle, the vulture, the raven, the ostrich and the owl, nor the seagull, the hawk, the heron, the swan nor the ibis nor the pelican, the hornbill, the water-hen and the bat; these are unclean. Ye shall not eat the locust nor the grasshopper nor anything of its kind for they are unclean and ye shall not touch their dead bodies, and whosoever touches them shall be unclean until the evening.

These things we have declared unto you in order that ye may keep and perform the Law of God so that ye may be blessed in this country, which God hath given unto you because of the heavenly Zion, the Tabernacle of the Law of God... it is because of Zion that ye have been chosen and our fathers rejected.

As for thee my Queen, thy wisdom is great and it surpasses the wisdom of men. There is none that can be compared with thee in respect of thy intelligence, and the understanding of thy heart is deeper than that of men, except my lord Solomon.

But thy wisdom so far exceedeth that of Solomon that thou hast been able to draw the mighty men of Israel and the Tabernacle of the Law of God with thy skill and thine understanding. Thou hast overthrown the house of their idols and destroyed their images and cleaned what was unclean among thy people, for thou hast driven away from them that which God hateth.

And as concerning thy name, God Himself hath prepared it, for He hath called thee *Makeda* which interpreted means 'Not thus'... 'Not thus' to worship the sun, but it is right to worship God. 'Not thus' to practise the working of magic, but to lean upon the Holy One of Israel. 'Not thus' to offer up sacrifices to idols of stone and wood, but it is right to offer up sacrifices unto God."

And it came to pass by the Will of God, that Zion hath come into this country of Ethiopia to be a guide to our king David II (Menyelek), the lover of God, the guardian of her Tabernacle, and the director of the habitation of his glory."

80. HOW THE KINGDOM OF BAYNA-LEHKEM (DAVID II, MENYELEK I) WAS ESTABLISHED IN ETHIOPIA

Then Azariah said: "Bring hither the jubilee trumpets and let us go to Zion, and there we will make new the kingdom of our lord, David." And he took the oil of sovereignty and filled the horn and he anointed David with the unguent, with the oil of sovereignty.

And they blew horns and pipes and trumpets, and beat drums, and sounded all kinds of musical instruments, and there was singing, dancing, games and displays with horses and all the men and women of the country of Ethiopia were present, small and great, and the pygmies, six thousand in number, also virgin women whom Azariah had chosen as the women of Zion whom David the King had destined to serve at the table and the banquets in the royal fortress whenever he went up there clad in raiment of fine gold.

So, in this manner was renewed the kingdom of David II (Menyelek I) the son of Solomon the King of Israel, in the capital city Dabra Makeda, in the House of Zion, when the Law was established for the first time by the King of Ethiopia.

Thus the eastern boundary of the kingdom of the King of Ethiopia is the beginning of the city of Gaza in the land of Judah and Jerusalem, and its boundary is the Lake of Jericho passing by the coast of its sea to Leba and Saba, bound by Bisis and Asnet.

Its other boundary is the Sea of the Black and Naked Men, going up to Mount Kebereneyon into the Sea of Darkness, that is, the place where the sun setteth, extending to Feneel and Lasifala, and its borders are the lands near the Garden of Paradise where there is plenty food and abundance of cattle; this boundary extendeth as far as Zawel and passeth on to the Sea of India with its boundary as far as the Sea of Tarsis. In its remote part lieth the Sea of Medyam, until it cometh to the country of Gaza.

So then, this is the extent of all the dominion of the King of Ethiopia and it belongeth to him and to his seed, for ever.

81. HOW THE MEN OF ROME DESTROYED THE FAITH

After waiting for three months, Zion came into the country of Ethiopia at the beginning of the first month in the language of the Hebrews. Then they wrote down the Law and the names, and deposited it as a memorial for later days, so that what was right should be done for the Tabernacle of Zion, that the glory of the Kings of Rome might be well known.

For the Kings of Ethiopia and the Kings of Rome were brethren and held the Christian faith, and believed in the preaching of the gospel up to the time of Constantine the Great and Helena the Queen, who brought forth the wood of the cross... *and the kings of Rome continued to believe for one hundred and thirty years.*

Then Satan, who hath been the enemy of man from of old, rose up and seduced the people of the country of Rome, and they corrupted the Faith of Christ, and they introduced heresies in the Church of God by the mouth of Nestorius and Arius, into whose hearts he cast the same jealousy as he had cast into the heart of Cain to slay his brother Abel.

In like manner did their father the Devil, the enemy of righteousness and the hater of good, cast jealousy even as David said: "They speak violence in the heights of heaven, and set their mouth in the heavens, and their tongue wags on the earth."[1]

Those same men who know not whence they came, and know not whither they are going, insult their Creator with their tongues and blaspheme His glory, while He is God the Word.

He came down from the throne of His Godhead and put on the body of Adam... and in that body He was crucified so that He might redeem Adam from his iniquity... then He went up into the heavens and sat upon the throne of His Godhead in that body which He had taken. And He shall come again in glory to judge the living and the dead, and shall reward every man according to his work.

82. THE FIRST WAR OF THE KING OF ETHIOPIA

After three months David II and his soldiers rose up to wage war from the city of the government, with Queen Makeda his mother and the Tabernacle Zion, his Lady.

And the Levites carried the Tabernacle of the Law while the other mighty men of war of Israel marched before it and behind it, and on the left side and on the right side of it. As in the times of old when God on Mount Sinai made Zion to come down in holiness to Moses and Aaron, even so did Azariah and Almeyas bear along the Tabernacle of the Law, singing psalms and songs of the spirit like the heavenly hosts, for God had given them beautiful voices and marvellous songs, as He was well pleased to be praised by them.

Then they came from the city of the government and encamped at Maya Abaw, and on the following morning they laid waste the district of Zawa, since enmity existed between them from olden time; and they blotted out the people and slew them with the edge of the sword.

---

[1]Psalm 73:6-9

After this they passed on from that place and encamped at Gerra, and here also they laid waste the city of vipers that had the faces of men and the tails of asses attached to their loins.

The Queen then returned and encamped in the city of Zion and they remained there three months, then their chariots moved on and came to the city of the government. Then in one day they came to the city of Saba, and they laid waste the district of Noba, then they encamped round about Saba and they laid it waste as far as the border of Egypt.

The majesty of the King of Ethiopia was so great that the King of Medyam and the King of Egypt caused gifts to be brought unto him. Then, when they encamped in Abat they waged war on the country of India, and the King of India brought gifts and did homage to the King of Ethiopia.

King David II waged war wherever he pleaseth, and no man conquered him, but whosoever attacked him was conquered, for Zion himself made the strength of the enemy to be exhausted. But King David II with his armies and all those who obeyed his word, ran by the chariots without pain, hunger or thirst, without sweat and exhaustion, and travelling in one day a distance that took three months to traverse.

And they lacked nothing whatsoever of the things which they asked God through the Tabernacle of the Law of God to give them, for He dwelt with her and His Angel directed her; for she was His habitation.

When the King wished something to be done, everything that he wished for and thought about in his heart and indicated with his finger, was performed at his word, and everyone feared him, but he feared no one, for the hand of God was with him and it protected him by day and by night.

He did God's will and God worked for him and protected him from all evil.

83. HOW THE AUTHORITY OF BAYNA-LEHKEM WAS UNIVERSALLY ACCEPTED

By the KEBRA NAGAST we know and have learned that most certainly the King of Ethiopia is honourable... *that he is the King of Zion, the firstborn of the seed of Shem... that the habitation of God is in Zion, and that He breaketh the might and power of all his enemies and foes... and that after him the King of Rome was the anointed of the Lord because of the wood of the Cross.*

Concerning the Kingdom of Israel, truly the Pearl was born of them, and of the Pearl was born the Sun of Righteousness Who hid Himself in the woman's body... for otherwise He could not have been seen by mortal eyes; and having put on our body He became like unto us, and He walked about with men.

He performed signs and wonders in their midst... He raised their dead, He opened the ears of their deaf and He cleansed the lepers; He satisfied the hungry with food, and He performed many of the miracles, some of which are written down and some of which are not.

When the wicked children of Israel saw all this they thought that He was a man, and they were envious of Him because of what they saw and heard, and they crucified Him upon the wood of the Cross and they killed Him. But He rose from the dead on the third day and went up into heaven in glory, and sat on the throne of the Godhead.

There He received from God a Kingdom incorruptible for ever and ever over the beings of spirit and the beings of earth, and over every created being, so that every tongue shall adore His Name, and every knee shall bow to Him; and He shall judge the living and the dead and reward every man according to his work.

Therefore when the Jews shall see Him they shall be put to open shame, and be condemned to the fire which is everlasting. But we who believe shall be upon our thrones and we shall rejoice with our teachers the Apostles, provided that we have walked in the way of Christ and in His commandments.

After the Jews had Crucified the Saviour of the world, they were scattered abroad, and their kingdom was destroyed, and they were subdued and rooted out for ever and ever.

Then all the saints who were gathered together said: *"In all truth the King of Ethiopia is more exalted and more honourable than any other king upon the earth, because of the glory and the greatness of the heavenly Zion.*

And God loveth the people of Ethiopia, for without knowing about His Law, they destroyed their idols; but those unto whom the Law of God had been given (the Jews), made idols and worshipped the false gods which God hateth.

When in later times He was born of the flesh to redeem Adam, He manifested signs and wonders before them, but they did not believe in Him nor in His teaching... whereas the people of Ethiopia believed in one trustworthy disciple, and for this reason God greatly loves the people of Ethiopia. He loves them with an undying and an everlasting love.

The seed of Abraham hath exalted the seed of Shem... they are all kings upon the earth, but the chosen ones of the Lord are the people of Ethiopia, for there rests the habitation of God, the heavenly Zion, the Tabernacle of His Law and of His Covenant, which He hath made into a mercy-seat through His love for the children of men; also for the rains and the waters from the skies, for the planted things and the fruits, for the peoples and the countries, the kings and nobles, for men and beasts, and for birds and creeping things."

Verily, salvation hath been given unto all of us who have believed in our Lady Mary, the likeness of the heavenly Zion, for the Lord dwelt in the womb of the Virgin, and was brought forth by her without carnal union. And the Ten Words of the Law were written by the Finger of God and placed in Zion, the Tabernacle of the Law of God.

And now we will declare from the Law of Moses the prophecies of the Prophets our Fathers, the holy men of olden times, and the prophecies concerning Christ our Redeemer, so that the generations of posterity may hear the narrative of the story, and we will also relate unto them the interpretation of the scripture.

We will begin then with the beginning of the book, and will make you to understand in the spirit, as David saith, through the Holy Spirit: 'In the beginning the book was written because of me.'[1]

And one answered and said: "What is the beginning of the Book?" And they answered and said unto him: " It is the Law which was written concerning Christ, the Son of God, 'In the beginning God made the heavens and the earth;'[2] and they existed from olden time. Then the earth was formless and there were mixed together darkness, winds, water, mist and dust; all of these were mixed together, and the Spirit of God hovered above the waters.

This means that by the Word of God the heavens and the earth were created, and these words mean that the Spirit of God dwelt over all creation."

[1]Psalm 40:7   [2]Genesis 1:1

PART V

The Seed Of The Woman

And the dragon was wroth with the woman,
and went to make war with the remnant of her seed,
which keep the Commandments of God,
and have the testimony of Jesus Christ.

Revelation 12:17

84. THE PROPHECY ABOUT CHRIST

Moses proclaimed in the Law and said: "A prophet like myself shall rise up for you from your brethren, and hearken ye unto him, and every soul that will not hearken unto that prophet ye shall root out from among the people."[1]

This he said concerning Christ the Son of God; and he also prophesied concerning His crucifixion, saying: "When the serpents afflicted the children of Israel they cried out to Moses, and Moses cried out to God to deliver them from the serpents."

Then God said unto him: "Make an image of a serpent in brass and suspend it in a place where it can be seen as a sign, and let every one whom a serpent hath bitten look upon that image of brass, and he shall live." Thus when they failed to look at it they died, and those who looked on it and believed lived.[2]

In like manner it was with Christ; those who paid no heed to Him and did not believe in Him perished in hell, and those who believed and hearkened unto Him, inherited the land of everlasting life, where there will never be pain or suffering.

And now we will make known unto you how they paid no heed to Christ, the Word of God.

The children of Israel spoke against Moses, saying: "Is it that God hath spoken to Moses only? How is it that we also do not hear the Word of God that we may believe on Him?"[3]

And God, Who knoweth the hearts of men, heard the murmuring of the children of Israel, and said unto Moses: "Thou asketh forgiveness for thy people, and yet they murmur against you, saying, why does not God speak with us also? So now, if they believe in Me, let them come to Me with thee. And tell them to purify themselves and to wash their garments, and let the great men of Israel go up to hear what commands I will give them. Let them hear My Voice and perform the Commandments which I shall give them."

---

[1]Compare Deuteronomy 18:15   [2]Numbers 21:7   [3]Numbers 12:2

Then Moses told the Children of Israel what he had been commanded, and the people bowed low before God, and they purified themselves on the third day. And the seventy elders of Israel[1] went up into Mount Sinai and they were distant from each other the space of a flight of an arrow, while they stood still, each facing his neighbour. Thus there were many of them, yet they were not able to ascend into the cloud with Moses, and fear and trembling seized upon them, and the shadow of death enveloped them... then they heard the sound of the horn and pipes and felt the darkness and winds.

When Moses went into the cloud and held converse with God, all the great men of Israel heard the Voice of God and they were afraid and quaked with terror, and because of the overwhelming fear that was in their hearts, they were unable to stand up.

But when Moses came forth they said unto him: "We will not hear this Word of God so that we may not die of terror. And behold, we know that God speaks with thee, so then if there be anything that He would say unto us, do thou listen and declare it unto us. Be unto us a mouth in respect of God, and we will be unto Him His own people."

Do ye not see that they denied Christ saying: "We will not listen to that Voice so that we may not die in terror"? For Christ is the Word of God, and therefore when they said: "We will not listen to that Voice," they meant: "We do not believe in Christ."

Again Moses spoke unto God and said: "Show me Thy Face."[2] And God said unto Moses: "No one can look upon My Face and live, but only as in a mirror. Turn thy face to the west and thou shalt see on the rock the reflection of My Face." When Moses saw the shadow of the Face of God, his own face shone with a brightness which was seven times brighter than the sun, and the light was so strong that the Children of Israel could not look upon his face except through a veil.

Moses saw that they did not desire to look upon the Face of God, for they said unto him: "Make unto us a veil so that we may see thy face."[3]

---

[1]Numbers 11:16-24; Exodus 33:18-23   [2]Exodus 33:18-23   [3]Exodus 34:33

Having said these words, it is evident that they hate the hearing of His Word and the sight of His Face.

Moreover, when Abraham took his son Isaac up into Mount Carmel, God sent down from heaven a ram for the redemption of Isaac. And Isaac was not slaughtered. Abraham is to be interpreted as God the Father, and Isaac is to be interpreted as a symbol of Christ the Son.

And when He came down from heaven for the salvation of Adam and his sons, the Godhead which had come down from heaven was not slain, only His body was slain, the Godhead suffering in no wise and remaining unchanged. So then, the mortal become living in the resurrection with the Godhead.

Now it is clearly manifest that Christ the Son of God hath redeemed us... He hath magnified us men... and we must honour especially, both upon the earth and in heaven, this our Lady Mary the Virgin, the Mother of God, the Second Zion.

Hearken ye now to this explanation concerning the first man, who is our father Adam. Eve was created from a bone in his side, without carnal embrace or union, and she became his companion. But having heard the word of deception, from being the help meet of Adam she became a murderess by making him to transgress the command.

But in his mercy God the Father created the Pearl in the body of Adam; He cleansed Eve's body and sanctified it and made it into a dwelling for Adam's salvation. Thus Mary was born without blemish, for He made her pure without pollution, and she redeemed his debt without carnal union and embrace.

She brought forth in heavenly flesh a King, and He was born of her, and he renewed His life in the purity of His body. He slew death with His pure body, and he rose without corruption raising us up with him to immortality, to the throne of divinity, and he hath raised us up to Him, and we have exchanged life in our mortal bodies and found a life which is immortal. Through the transgression of Eve we died and were buried, and by the purity of Mary we received honour, and are exalted to the heights.

135

Ezekiel also prophesied concerning Mary, saying: "I saw a door in the east which was sealed with a great and marvellous seal, and there was none who went into it except the Lord of hosts; He went into it and came forth therefrom."[1]

Hear ye now this explanation. When he saith: "I saw a door," it was the door of the gate of heaven, the entrance of the saints into the kingdom of the heavens. And when he saith: "It was in the east," he refers to her purity and her beauty. Men call her the "gate of salvation," and also "the East" unto whom the saints look to with joy and gladness.

The "closeness" of which he speaks refers to her virginity and her body; and when he said that she was sealed with "a great and wonderful seal" this showeth plainly that she was sealed by God, the Great and Wonderful, through the Holy Ghost.

Moreover, when he said: "None goeth through it except the Lord of host, He goeth in and cometh out," he means the Creator of the heavens and the earth, of angels, men and lords. The Lord of Hosts is the fruit of the Godhead, Who put on our body from her, Christ. He went into and came forth from her without polluting her.

Moses also prophesied concerning Mary, saying: "I saw a bramble bush on Mount Sinai which the devouring fire consumed not,"[2] and the meaning of this fire is the Godhead of the Son of God; and the bramble bush, which burned without the leaves thereof being consumed, is Mary.

85. THE MURMURING OF ISRAEL

Once again the Children of Israel murmured concerning the ministration of the priest before the Lord, saying: "Are we not Israel, of the seed of Abraham? Why cannot we also offer up sacrifice like them in the Tent of Witness by the Tabernacle of the Law of God, the holy Zion, with censers and incense and the holy instrument? Why should Moses

---

[1]Ezekiel 43:1   [2]Exodus 3:2

and his brother Aaron and their children alone do this? Are we not people whom God hath chosen as much as them?" And when Moses heard this he said unto them: "Do ye whatsoever ye will."

Then the elders of Israel went and made seventy censers with which they would perfume Zion and praise God, and they took incense and coals in the censers, and went into the Holy of Holies to offer up incense, but immediately after placing the incense into the censers, at the first swing of them fire came forth from the censers and they themselves were burnt up completely and melted away.

As wax melteth before the face of the fire, even so did they melt away; and as grass withereth away when flame approaches it even so were they consumed together with their instruments, and there was nothing left of them except their censers. And God said: "Sanctify to Me these censers for My Tent, and they shall be used for My offerings, for they were consecrated by the death of those men."[1]

The censer is Mary. . . and Christ, the Son of God, the Godhead, is the coals, and the odour of the incense is the perfume of the righteousness of Christ, and through Him also the perfume of His Apostles, Prophets and Martyrs who have rejected the world and inherited the Kingdom of Heaven. The chains of the censers are the ladder which Jacob saw, to which the angels clung as they went up and came down; and upon the perfume of the incense the prayers of the pure in heart go up to the throne of God. When the flame had burned up the sinners, the people who were kinsmen of those who had been destroyed reviled Moses and Aaron, and said unto them: "Ye have made our elders to perish"; and they took up stones to stone Moses and Aaron. [2]

But God was exceedingly angry with Israel and He scorned as a filthy rag the counsel of Dathan and Abiram, the sons of Korah. Then the Word of God made a sign to the earth and the earth opened her mouth and swallowed them up, together with all their companions, their wives, their children and their beasts. They went down into Sheol (hell) alive, and the earth shut herself up over them. . . As for the people who had been associated with them and had heard the revilings upon Moses, God sent upon them a plague, and they died forthwith.

---

[1]Numbers 16   [2]Compare Exodus 17:4 and Numbers 16:41

Moses and Aaron came with incense and censers, and they wept before God, and entreated Him for forgiveness for the people, saying: "Remember, O Lord, Abraham Thy friend and Isaac Thy servant, and Israel Thy Holy one... for we are their seed and the children of Thy people. Cool Thy wrath in respect of us, and make haste to hear us... Destroy us not and remove Thy punishment from upon Thy people." And God the Merciful saw the sincerity of Moses, and had compassion upon them.

Then God spoke unto Moses, and said unto him: "Speak thou to this people and say unto them: 'Sanctify ye yourselves, and bring ye for each of the houses of your father a rod,' then write ye upon it so that ye may know their rods, thou and thy brother Aaron. Of your houses let Aaron write upon his rod, but upon thine own rod make no mark, for it shall be a perfect miracle for the children of thy people, and a vindication from the wicked and a sign of life for all those who believe."

86. THE ROD OF MOSES AND THE ROD OF AARON

Moses spoke these words unto them, and they brought a rod into each of the houses of their fathers which they had chosen for purity, and so there were twelve rods. And Moses wrote upon their rods the names of their fathers: on the rod of Aaron was written the name of Levi, on the rod of Adonyas was written the name of Reuben, and on the rod of every man of all the houses of Israel was written in like manner the name of his father.

And God said unto Moses: "Carry the rods of Zion to the Tent of Witness, and shut them up therein until the morning, then take them out before the men and give unto each of them his rod, according to the houses of their fathers whose names are written on the rods, and the man on whose rod a mark shall be found... it is he whom I have chosen to be priest to Me."

Moses told the people these words and they did according as God had commanded them. Then when the morning had come, Moses took the rods, and all the elders of Israel and Aaron also came. And Moses came before them and he lifted up the rods and brought them before all the people, *and the rod of Aaron was found with the fruit and flower of an almond which emitted a fragrant perfume.* And Moses said unto them: "Look ye now. This is the rod which the Lord your God hath chosen... fear ye Him and worship Him;" and all the people bowed down before God.

This rod is Mary. And the rod which, without water, burst into bloom indicates also Mary, from whom was born without the seed of man, the Word of God. And when he said: "I have chosen, I will make manifest a miracle, and he shall be priest to Me;" it means that God chose Mary out of all the congregation of Israel, even as David her father prophesied saying: "The Lord loveth the gates of Zion more than all the habitations of Jacob,"[1] and he further said: "Marvellous is His speech concerning thee, O city of God."[2]

Thus, when he said: "More than all the habitations of Israel" and "her gates" he refers to the silence of her mouth, the purity of her lips and the praise which goeth forth from her mouth, like honey which floweth from her lips, and the purity of her virginity which was without spot or blemish or impurity before she brought forth; and after she had brought forth she was pure and holy, and so shall it be even as it was, unto all eternity.

And in the heavens she goeth about with the angels, a pure thing...and she is the rod of Aaron. Thus she liveth in Zion with the pot which is filled with manna, and with the two tables of stone that were written with the Finger of God. But the heavenly, spiritual Zion is above them, the holy Zion, the making and constitution of which are wonderful, and of which God Himself is her Maker and Fashioner, a true habitation of His glory.

And God again spoke unto Moses saying: "Make a Tabernacle of wood which is indestructible by worms and rot, and cover it over with plates of fine gold, every part thereof."[3] The gold is the fineness of the Godhead that came down from heaven... and in like manner is plated with gold the Tabernacle, the abode of the heavenly Zion.

---

[1]Psalm 87:2   [2]Psalm 87:3   [3]Exodus 25:10 "an ark of shittim wood"

The Tabernacle is to be interpreted as Mary, and the wood which is indestructible is to be interpreted as Christ our Redeemer; and again the pot of gold inside the Tabernacle,[1] is to be interpreted as Mary, and the manna which is in the pot is to be interpreted as the body of Christ which came down from heaven, and the Word of God which is written upon the two tables is to be interpreted as Christ, the Son of God. The spiritual Zion then, is to be interpreted as the light of the Godhead.

The spiritual Pearl which is contained in the Tabernacle is like a brilliant gem of great price, and he who has acquired it holds it tightly in his hand, and while the gem is in his hand its owner goeth into the Tabernacle, and he is a priest therein. He who possesseth the Pearl is to be interpreted as the Word of God, Christ, and the spiritual Pearl which is grasped is to be interpreted as Mary, the Mother of the Light, through whom "Christos", the "Unmixed", assumed a body.

In her He made a temple for Himself of her pure body, and from her was born the Light of all Lights Who was born of His own free will and was not made by another, but He made a Temple for Himself through an incomprehensible wisdom which transcends the mind of man.

When God brought Israel out of Egypt, they thirsted for water in Kades and they murmured and wept before Moses, and Moses went to God with their laments. And God said unto him: "Take thy rod and strike this rock."[2] And Moses struck the rock in length and breadth in the form of the Cross and water flowed forth in twelve streams. And they drank their fill of the water, the people and their beasts, and when they had drunk, that rock followed after them.

The rock is to be interpreted as Christ, the streams of water as the Apostles , that which they drank as the teaching of the gospel, and the rod as the wood of the Cross. And that rock is firm: "He who buildeth upon a rock shall not be moved by the demons."[3] And again He said ''I am the door."[4]

---

[1]Exodus 16:33 "take a pot and put an omer of manna therein"
[2]Exodus 17:6
[3]Matthew 7:24-25
[4]John 10:7-9

"Thou art the rock," He said unto Peter. "And upon thee I will build the Christian people."[1] And again he said: "I am the Shepherd of the sheep[2] and he said unto him thrice: "Feed my sheep."[3] And again He said: "I am the stem of the vine... Ye are its branches and its clusters of fruit."[4]

The rod of Moses by means of which he performed the miracle is to be interpreted as the wood of the Cross, with which he delivered Adam and his children from the punishments of devils.

As Moses smote the water of the river and turned it into blood and slew their fish, in like manner Christ slew death with His Cross and brought them out of Sheol. And as Moses smote the air with his rod and the whole land of Egypt became dark for three days and three nights[5] with darkness which could be felt, so that the Egyptians could not rise from their beds, so Christ, being crucified upon the Cross, brightened the darkness of the hearts of men and rose up from the dead on the third day.

And as the rod of Moses changed itself and transformed itself by the Word of God,[6] being dry yet possessing life, and possessing life yet becoming a dry thing, even so Christ with the wood of the Cross made life for the people who believe on Him, and with the Sign of the Cross made them to drive away devils.

Verily, demons and Christians became changed. The spiritual beings became reprobates and through transgressing the commandment of their Lord they became exiled ones by the might of His Cross. But we have become spiritual beings through receiving His Body and Blood, in place of those spiritual beings who were exiled, and we are now souls worthy of praise who have believed in His Cross and His Resurrection.

Therefore, as Moses smote the mountains by stretching out his hands with his rod, and brought forth punishments by the command of God, even so Christ drove out the demons from men by the might of His Cross. When God said unto Moses: "Smite with the rod," He meant: "Make the Sign of the Cross of Christ," and when God said unto Moses:

---

[1]Matthew 16:18   [2]John 10:11,14   [3]John 21:17
[4]John 15:5,16   [5]Exodus 10:21-22   [6]Exodus 7:10

"Stretch out thy hand,"[1] He meant that by the spreading out of His hand Christ hath redeemed us from the servitude of the enemy and hath given us life by the stretching out of His hand upon the wood of the Cross.

When Amalek fought with Israel, Moses went up into the mountain, and Aaron was with him. They went up to pray because Amalek was prevailing. And God commanded Moses and said unto him: "Stretch out thy hand until Israel gets power over Amalek."[2]

The hands of Moses were held out until sunset, but they became heavy and he being weary dropped his hands, and then Israel ceased to prevail and their enemies overcame them. But when Moses kept his hands out straight Amalek was overcome… and Israel put to flight and vanquished their enemy Amalek.

When Aaron and Hur saw this they piled up stones on the right and on the left of Moses, and they made the hand of Moses to rest on the stones which they had built up, and Aaron on his right and Hur on his left held Moses with their shoulders, so that his hands might not drop from their stretched out position.

---

[1]Exodus 7:19   [2]Exodus 17:11-12

The war of Amalek against Israel is the war of believers against demons, and before Christ was crucified the demons had conquered the believers. But when he stretched out his hands on the wood of the Cross because of the sin of Adam and his children, and his palm was pierced with nails, those who were sealed with the Sign of the Cross of Christ conquered the demons.

The stretching out of the hands of Moses symbolizes the Cross of Christ; and that Aaron and Hur piled up stones indicates the wood of the Cross and the nails. Also, Aaron represents the thief on the right and Hur the thief on the left. Then Amalek represents the demons, and the king of Amalek symbolizes Satan. As concerning that the Amalekites were conquered, this signifies that we have conquered demons and Satan by the Resurrection of Christ and by His Cross.

When Israel went out of bondage in Egypt, they came to bitter water which they could not drink, and they lamented because of the bitterness of the water. And God said unto Moses: "Lift up thy rod and cast it into the water,[1] and sign it with the sign of the Cross right and left." Had God said unto him: "Let it become sweet," then the water would have become sweet. But He made manifest that by the Sign of the Cross of Jesus Christ every polluted thing becometh good and pleasant.

So now, I will declare unto thee from the prophets concerning His Crucifixion. David said: "They have pierced my hands and my feet."[2]

And again He said: "They made Me drink vinegar for my thirst."[3] The Breath of Life that had breathed upon Adam drank vinegar, and the Hand that had made the earth was pierced with a nail. He who for the sake of Adam abased Himself, was born and took the form of a servant.

87. PARABLE OF THE TWO SLAVES (THE DEVIL AND ADAM)

A certain king had two slaves; one was arrogant and strong, and the other was humble and weak. And the arrogant overcame the humble one and smote him and all but killed him, and robbed him, and the king

---

[1]Compare Exodus 15:25   [2]Psalm 22:16   [3]Psalm 69:21

upon his throne saw them. And the king descended and seized the arrogant slave, beat him and crushed him, bound him in fetters and cast him into a place of darkness.

Then he raised up his humble and weak slave, embraced him and brushed away the dust from him, washed him and poured oil and wine on his wounds and set him upon his horse and brought him into his city; and he set him upon his throne and seated him on his right hand.

The king is in truth Christ, th arrogant servant is Satan, and the humble servant is Adam. When Christ saw how the arrogant servant overcame the humble one and cast him upon the ground, He came down from His throne and raised up Adam His servant, and bound Satan in fetters and in the terror of Sheol.

Then He seated the body of Adam upon the throne of his Godhead, and magnified him and exalted him, and honoured him; and he was praised by all the beings whom He had created, the angels and the archangels, thousands and tens of thousands of spiritual beings. For He brought down low the arrogant one and rose up the humble.

He reduced the arrogant to shame and exalted to honour the humble. He rejected the arrogant and loved the humble, and He scorned the haughty and had pity on the lowly... He cast down the arrogant from this high place, and lifted up the poor out of the dust. He snatched away the mighty one from his honour, and raised up the poor from corruption, for with Him are honour and disgrace. Whom He wisheth to honour He honoureth, and whom He wisheth to disgrace He disgraceth.

88. HOW THE ANGELS REBELLED AGAINST GOD WHEN HE CREATED ADAM

There were certain angels with whom God was wroth (He the Knower of hearts knew them), for they reviled Adam, saying: "God hath shown love to him and hath set us to minister unto him... likewise the beasts and creeping things, the fish of the sea, the birds of the air and all fruits... the trees of the field, the heavens and the earth also. He hath appointed the heavens to give him rain and the earth to give him fruits.

The sun and the moon also hath He given him, the sun to give him light by day and the moon to give him light by night. He hath fashioned him with His own fingers and He hath created him in His own image; He kissed him and breathed into him spirit of life, and He said unto him, 'My son, My firstborn, My beloved.' And He set him in a garden to eat and enjoy himself without sickness or suffering and without toil and labour, but He hath commanded him not to eat from one tree. And being given all these things by God, Adam transgressed and ate of that tree... and he became hated and rejected, and God drove him out of the garden; since that time Adam, abandoned his hope, for he transgressed the commandment of his Creator."

Then God answered the angels who reviled Adam and He said unto them: "Why do ye revile Adam in this manner? For he is flesh and blood, ashes and dust." And the angels answered and said unto him: "May we declare before Thee the sin of Adam?" And God said unto them: "Declare ye his sin and I will hearken unto you, and I Myself will answer you in respect of Adam My servant." For God loved His son, Adam.

And God said: "I created him out of the dust, and I will not cast away that which I have fashioned. I brought him out of non-existence, and I will not make My handiwork a laughing stock for his enemies." And those angels responded, saying: "Praise be unto Thee, O Lord. For Thou, the Knower of hearts, knowest that we have reviled Adam because he transgressed Thy commandment, that he was not to eat of one tree after Thou hast made him lord over everything which Thou hast created, and hath set him over every work of Thy hands.

If Thou had not told him, and if Thou had not commanded him not to eat of one tree, there would have been no offence on his part; and if he had eaten because of a lack of food there would have been no offence on his part.

But thy word made him to know, and Thou hadst said: 'As surely as thou eatest of this tree thou shalt die.'[1] Yet he after hearing this became

---

[1]Genesis 2:17

bold and ate. Thou didst not let him lack sweet fruits to eat from the Garden, and Thou didst not let him lack one to comfort him... a companion like unto himself. So then, these things we say and make known unto Thee, and we have declared unto Thee how he hath transgressed Thy commandment."

Then the Merciful One, the Lover of Mankind, answered them on behalf of Adam, and said unto them: "You have I created out of fire and air with the one intent that ye should praise Me. Him have I created of twice as many elements as you; of dust and water, and of wind and fire; and he became a being of flesh and blood. And in him are ten thoughts or intentions; five good and five evil. If his heart incites him to good, then he walks with good intent; but if the devil seduces him, he walketh with him on an evil path.

As for you, ye have no other object in your minds but praise of Me, with the exception of that arrogant one who produced evil and became an evil being, and was driven forth from your assembly. And now... why do ye magnify yourselves over Adam? If ye were as he is, and I had created you of water and dust also, ye would have been flesh and blood and ye would have transgressed My commandment more than he hath done, and denied My word."

And the angels said unto Him: "Praise be unto Thee O Lord! Far be it from us! We will not transgress Thy commandment, and we will not oppose Thy word, for we are spiritual beings for life and he is a creature of dust, doomed to folly. So now try us well, and put us to the test so that Thou mayest know whether we are able to keep Thy word."

When the angels had exalted themselves in this manner, God, the Lover of Mankind, said unto them: "If ye go astray in transgressing My word, the wrong will be upon your own heads, then hell, fire and sulphur, fervent heat and whirlwind shall be your habitation until the Great Day... And ye shall be kept in chains which can neither be loosened nor broken for ever. But if ye keep truly My word and do My commandment, ye shall sit at My right hand and at My left hand... for everyone who hath conquered is mighty, and he who is conquered shall be overpowered.

Satan hath no power whatsoever, for he hath only what he maketh to germinate in the mind. He cannot grasp firmly nor perform anything, he cannot beat and he cannot drag away, he cannot seize and he cannot fight; he can only make thoughts to develop silently in the mind. Then him who is caught by the evil mind, he prepareth for destruction; but if a man hath conquered the evil mind he findeth grace and hath a reward which is everlasting.

And now, according to what ye wish there shall be upon you the mind of a man and the body of a man. But take good heed to yourselves that ye transgress not My word and break not My commandment; and defile not yourselves with eating, drinking, fornication, or with any other evil thing whatsoever; and transgress ye not My word."

Immediately there were given unto them by His word, flesh and blood, and a heart like the children of men. And those angels were pleased to leave the heights of heaven… and they came down to earth, to the folly of the dancing of the children of Cain with all their man-made idols which they had made in the folly of their fornication, and to their singing which they accompanied with the tambourine, flutes, pipes, and much shouting and loud cries of joy and noisy songs.

The daughters of men were there and they enjoyed the orgies without shame, for they scented themselves for the men who pleased them, and they lost the balance of their minds. The men did not restrain themselves for a moment, but they took from among the women those whom they desired, and they committed unspeakable abominations with them.[1]

God was wroth with them, so He bound them in the terror of Sheol until the day of redemption; as the Apostle said: "He treated His angels with severity. He spared them not, but made them to dwell in a state of judgment, and they were chained until the Great Day."[2]

Thus the Word of God conquered; He had fashioned Adam in His likeness and image, and those who had reviled and made a laughing stock of Adam were conquered.

---

[1]Genesis 6:2   [2]II Peter 2:4

147

The daughters of Cain with whom the angels had sinned conceived, but they were unable to bring forth their children and they died. Of the children which were in their wombs, some died and some did come forth by splitting open the bellies of their mothers.

They came forth by their navels, and when they were grown up they became giants whose height reached into the clouds; but for their sake and the sake of sinners the wrath of God became quiet, and He said: "My Spirit shall only rest on them for one hundred and twenty years, then I will destroy them with the waters of the flood... them and all sinners who have not believed the Word of God."

To those who believed the word of their fathers and did His will, no injury came from the waters of the flood, but He delivered them, saying: "If thou believest My word thou canst save thyself from the flood." And Noah said: "O Lord, I believe Thy word, make me to know by what means I can be saved." And God said unto him: "Thou canst be saved from the water by wood." Then Noah said: "How, O Lord?"

And God said unto him: "Make thyself a four-sided ark and build it with the work of the carpenter, and make for it three storeys inside, and go into it with all thy house."[1]

Noah believed the word of God, made the ark and was saved. God could have given unto Noah wings like the eagle and transported him to the country of the living with all his household, until His anger with the sinners who had not believed the word of God had cooled; or He could have lifted him up into the air, or He could have commanded the water of the flood which was like a wall, not to approach the one mountain where He could make Noah to dwell with his sons, and not to submerge the beasts and cattle which he wanted.

But know ye this, *God was well pleased that by means of wood which had been sanctified, the salvation of His creation should take place...that is, through the ark and the wood of the Cross.*

---

[1]Genesis 6:14

148

God said unto Noah: "Make that whereby thou shalt be saved," that is to say, the Tabernacle of the Church; and when He said unto him: "Make it four-sided," He showed that the Sign of the Cross was fourfold.

The four corners of the ark are the horns of the altar... and He commanded Moses to make the ark (the Ark of the Covenant) out of indestructible wood. He said: "I will sanctify thee from filth, from impurity, fornication, vindictiveness and falsehood, together with thy brother and thy house. Now, sacrifice unto Me a clean sacrifice with cleanness, and I will accept thee after thou hast sanctified thyself and thy house; command all the people to sanctify themselves, for My holy things must be offered by holy ones.

And this thou shalt seek, the Tabernacle of My Covenant which I have created for My praise. Then, if ye come to Me with purity of heart, with love and peace, without mockery and reviling, and if ye will make right your hearts in respect of Me and your neighbour, I will hear your prayers, and I will listen to your petitions about everything which ye submit to Me, and I will come and be with you, and I will walk among you and I will dwell in your hearts, and ye shall be unto Me My people, and I will be your God in truth."

89. CONCERNING HIM THAT EXISTETH IN EVERYTHING

Again God said unto Moses: "Make for Me an open space before the courtyard of he Tabernacle; no man who is impure sexually and unclean shall come there, and no one who is not pure. For I am there, and not only there, but in every place where My name is invoked in purity.

I was with Daniel in the lion's den and I was with Jonah in the belly of the great fish. I stand under the deepest deep so that the mountains may not sink down upon the waters; and I am under the waters so that they may not sink down upon the fire and sulphur; I stand under the fire and sulphur so that they may not sink down upon the winds and the void.

I stand under the deepest darkness and under the abysses, and every created thing supports itself on Me, and everything which I have created cometh to me as a place of refuge.

I am above the earth and I am at the ends of the world... I am Master of everything. I am in the air, My place of abode, and I am above the chariot of the Cherubim, and I am praised everlastingly by all the angels and by holy men. I am above the heights of the heaven and I fill everything. I am above the Seven Heavens.

I see everything and I test everything, and there is no other god besides Me, neither in the heaven above nor in the earth beneath; there is none like unto Me, saith God. My hand hath laid the foundations of the earth and My right hand hath made strong the heavens; I and My Son and My Holy Spirit."

90. THE REJECTION OF THE WORD

Let us weep for them... for the wickedness of the iniquitous Jews. Woe be unto the Jews and unto pagans who have wandered from the truth and have refused to submit to the love of God, with which in His goodness He hath loved man. For after Adam was rejected through his sin, He saved him by the greatness of His mercy, being crucified on the wood of the Cross, His hands pierced with nails.

With His palms stretched out in humility and His head bowed to one side, He to whom suffering was unfitting, for our sakes suffered in the everlasting majesty of His Godhead. He died that He might destroy death; He suffered exhaustion that He might give strength to the weakened man of dust; being thirsty he drank vinegar and He was crowned with a crown of thorns.

He feared not and was not ashamed by the cunning, the hatred and the spitting of the polluted Jews. From them He suffered beatings and was punched with fists... He was pierced and transfixed with nails, He was mocked and reviled though He is God and the King of Death, He, the Bestower of Glory Who endured patiently all disgrace.

Wearied and miserable they made Him sad when they rejected Him and hated Him; yet strong and glorious, they saddened Him when they brought false charges against Him.

For He Himself knew His Godhead, He knew His glory and He knew Himself. And there was none who knew Him for He was the Creator of everything. If they had known Him they would not have crucified the Lord of Glory.

He had said in His Mercy: "Forgive them Father, for they know not what they do."[1] They thought their Creator was a created being, and so they slew the Man-God who did not belong to mortal creatures. He was not something that had been made by hands, but He Himself was the Maker and the Creator, Light of Lights, God of gods, Son of the Father, Jesus Christ.

Isaiah, the man of keen words among the prophets, said: "He was a humble man, and His appearance was rejected, like a root He hid Himself in parched ground, He came in the flesh as a being of the earth though He was the Sustainer and Saviour of the universe."[2]

Concerning the Jews, those enemies of the truth, He said: "I have called for them and they have not answered Me, I have loved them and they have hated Me."[3] And David had said: "They returned unto me evil for good, and they hated me in return for my love for them."[4] Again the prophet Isaiah said: "With their lips they profess love for me, but in their hearts they keep afar from me, and their worshipping of me is an empty thing."[5]

Thus God rewarded the Jews according to their wickedness and He treated the Gentiles according to their humility, for He is merciful and compassionate to those who call upon Him, who take refuge in Him, and who purify themselves from all uncleanness, also loving those who weep and repent.

Stephen had spoken unto the Jews whilst he was standing up to martyr-dom and the Jews were killing him with stones; and he said unto them as he showed them their folly in not having kept the commandments of God: "Ye have not kept the Law according to the ordinance of the

---

[1]Luke 23:24   [2]Isaiah 53:2   [3]Compare Psalm 45:5, 58:7
[4]Psalm 109:5   [5]Isaiah 29:13

angels, as ye received it." When they heard this they went mad with anger and gnashed their teeth.[1]

91. THE HORNS OF THE ALTAR

The Tabernacle symbolizes the horns of the altar where the holy priests offer up sacrifice, whereon they place the table, the similitude of the grave wherein Christ was buried in Golgotha.

On the table the offering is a symbol of the firstborn, the body of Immanuel, the "pure," the "unmixed" body which our Saviour took from Mary and of which He said unto His apostles: "Eat ye My Body;[2] whosoever eateth not of My Body hath no portion with Me and no everlasting life.

But he who hath eaten My Body, even though he be dead, shall live for ever, for he is associated with My Body and My Blood and he hath become My heir, and he shall say to My Father: 'Our Father which art in heaven,' and the Father shall answer him, saying: 'Thou art my Son'."

92. THE ARK OF NOAH AND THE TALK OF THE WICKED

God saved Noah in the Ark and God held converse with Abraham in the wood of Manbar,[3] the wood that cannot be destroyed, and He saved Isaac by means of the ram which was caught in the thicket[4] and He made Jacob wealthy by means of three rods of wood which he laid in running water,[5] and through the top of his staff Jacob was also blessed.[6] And he said unto Moses, "Make a tabernacle of wood which cannot be destroyed, make it in the similitude of Zion the Tabernacle of the Covenant." And when David took it from the city of Samaria, he placed the Tabernacle of the Law in a new abode and he rejoiced before it.[7]

---

[1]Acts 7:53, 54

[2]Matthew 26:26

[3]Compare Genesis 18:1 (Manbar or Mamre)

[4]Genesis 22:13

[5]Genesis 30:37-43

[6]Genesis 47:31; Hebrew 11:21

[7]II Samuel 6:3

From the beginning God had made the Tabernacle the means of salvation and many signs and wonders were performed through it, for God had ordained salvation through the wood of His Cross, in the Tabernacle of His Law, from the beginning to the end.

Salvation came unto Adam through the wood, as Adam's first transgression also came through the fruit of the wood. Those who come into His habitation and are accepted in the holy Tabernacle, and who pray unto Him with all their hearts, He will hear and will save in the day of their tribulation and He will fulfill their desire, for He hath made the holy Tabernacle to be a similitude of His throne.

The similitude and the fruit thereof are the Mother of the Redeemer, Mary. It is right that we should worship her, as in her name is blessed the Tabernacle of the Law of God. And it is right that we should worship Michael and Gabriel. When it was said unto Him: "Behold them, Thy father and Thy mother outside seeking Thee," Christ the Lover of Mankind answered and stretching out His hand towards those whom He was teaching, said: "Behold them, My father, My mother and My brother. Whosoever hath heard My word and hath done the Will of My Father, that same is My father and My mother and My sister."[1]

O Thou blind-hearted Jew, canst thou not see His Mercy and His love for humanity when He spake thus? He neither separated nor made a distinction, but He said unto them: "My brother"; for He loveth those who love Him and keep His commandments.

And now, we will declare unto you what is written concerning the pride of Pharaoh. Moses did as God commanded him and turned his rod into a serpent, and Pharaoh commanded the magicians and the sorcerers to do the same with their rods. And they made their rods into three serpents which by means of magic wriggled before Moses and Aaron, and before Pharaoh and the nobles of Egypt.

But the rod of Moses swallowed up the rods of the magicians, for those deceivers had worked magic for the sight of the eyes of men, not knowing that that which happens through the Word of God overcomes every king of magic that can be performed.

---

[1] Compare Matt. 12:49; Mark 3:34

153

93. THE BELIEF OF ABRAHAM

Abraham and David and all the prophets, one after the other, prophesied concerning the coming of the Son of God... and they were justified by faith. Abraham had said: "Wilt Thou in my days, O Lord, cast Thy word upon the ground?" And God said unto him: "By no means. His time hath not yet come, but I will show thee a similitude of His coming. Get thee over the Jordan, dip thyself in the water as thou goest over, and arrive at the city of Salem where thou shalt meet Melchizedek, and I will command him to show thee the sign and similitude of Him."

Abraham did this and he found Melchizedek and he gave him the mystery of the bread and wine,[1] that same which is celebrated in our Passover as a memorial of the sacrifice of our Lord Jesus Christ.

This was the desire and the joy of Abraham as he went round the altar which Melchizedek had made, carrying branch and palm on the day of the Sabbath. See how he rejoiced in his belief, and see how he was justified by his belief, O blind Jew, who though having eyes seest not, and having ears hearest not, even as the prophet Isaiah saith concerning you: "Their eyes are blind and their hearts are covered with darkness, so that they may not understand and God may not show compassion unto them."[2]

94. PROPHECIES CONCERNING THE COMING OF CHRIST

Isaiah the prophet prophesied concerning His coming, saying: "A son is born unto us. A child is given unto us. Dominion is written upon His shoulder. He is God, strong in rulership, King, great Counsellor is His Name."[3]

The meaning of this is manifest: the Son of God is born, whose sovereignty was written down before the world was, and He is wiser them anyone else.

---

[1]Genesis 14:18   [2]Compare Isaiah 6:10; 44:18   [3]Isaiah 9:6

Again Isaiah prophesied and said: "Behold My servant Whom I have chosen, on Whom is the delight of My soul, and the nations shall put their confidence in Him."[1] By these words we understand that Christ is the Spirit of God, the Word of the Father Who put on our flesh and was born for us; and the people of Rome and Ethiopia and all other nations have believed in Him.

And unto the people of Israel He spake and prophesied saying: "Many shall follow after Thee with their loins girded up and their backs bound with chains, and they shall pray to Thee and worship Thee, for Thou art God, and we have not recognized Thee."[2]

This he said because Israel had made itself blind and crucified Him, and refused to walk in His righteousness. Thus when Isaiah prophesied saying: "God shall come, and the heathen shall put their trust in Him and shall know Him"[3] he meant that Christ shall come and the Jews shall reject Him, but the heathen shall believe in Him.

Again he prophesied and said: "Be strong, ye weak hands and tired knees, and rejoice ye hearts that are cast down, for God hath come and shall blot out our debt and save us. He shall open the eyes of the blind and He shall make the ears of the deaf to hear; the feet that are lame shall run and the tongue of the dumb shall speak."[4]

These words are spoken in respect of those who sin by worshipping idols, and those who are dead in error and whose hearts are darkened, and of you who do not know that God created you.

Rejoice ye this day for He hath come who will redeem the sin of Adam, and make Adam's debt His own. He was crucified being sinless and He hath killed death by means of His own death. This is the meaning of this prophecy.

Of Him, David the Prophet prophesied and said: "God shall come in visible form, and our God will not keep silence."[5]

---

[1]Isaiah 42:1 [2]Compare Jeremiah 30:6-9 [3]Isaiah 60:2-3
[4]Isaiah 35:3 [5]Psalm 50:3

Also Jeremiah prophesied and said: "God shall come down upon the earth, and shall walk about with men like us."[1]

Then Ezekiel the prophet prophesied and said: "I your God will come, and I will walk about among them, and they shall know Me that I am their God."[2]

Again David prophesied and said: "Blessed is He who cometh in the name of God; we have blessed you in the name of the Lord."[3]

Solomon his son prophesied and said: "Verily God shall be with men, and He shall walk about upon the earth."[4]

And his father David hath prophesied, saying: "He shall come down like the dew upon wool, and like the drop which waters the earth, and righteousness shall spring into being in his days."[5]

And again Solomon, David's son, prophesied and said: "A Saviour shall be born out of Zion, and He shall remove all sin from Jacob…"[6]

Thus Micah the Prophet prophesied and said: "The Word of God shall appear in Jerusalem, and the Law shall go forth from Zion."[7]

And Zechariah the Prophet prophesied and said: "Rejoice, O daughter of Zion. Behold, I am alive, and I will dwell in thee, saith God, the Holy one of Israel."[8]

Thus prophesied David the Prophet, saying: "And He shall live, and they shall give Him of the gold of Arabia, and they shall pray for Him continually, and He shall be the strength of all the earth upon the tops of the mountains."[9]

Again Isaiah the Prophet prophesied, saying: "Behold, the virgin shall conceive and shall bring forth a Son, and she shall call His name Emmanuel."[10]

---

[1] Compare Jeremiah 32:38   [2]Ezekiel 11:17-20; 36:27-28 [3]Psalm 118:26
[4] Compare Zechariah 2:10-11 [5]Psalm 72:6-7   [6]Compare Isaiah 59:20
[7] Micah 4:2   [8]Zechariah 9:9   [9]Psalm 72:15
[10]Isaiah 7:14

Of Him David the Prophet prophesied, saying: "I brought thee forth from the womb before the star of the morning."[1] And again he said: "God said unto me: 'Thou art my Son, and I have this day brought thee forth'."[2] And again he said: "God looked down from heaven upon the children of men, and from the temple of His sanctuary."[3]

Moses the Prophet prophesied and said: "And all the children of God shall say, 'He is strong, for He will avenge the blood of his sons'."[4]

Thus David prophesied and said: "And there will I make the horn of David to rise up, and I will prepare a lamp for my anointed, and I will clothe his enemies with shame, and in him shall my holiness flourish.[5] Again David said: "A people whom I do not know shall serve me; at the first hearing of my word they shall answer me."[6] And to the Jews he said: "The children of the stranger have become old and have travelled proudly on their path. God liveth, and blessed is my God."[7]

When he saith unto thee: "God liveth," he speaketh of His Godhead; and when he saith unto thee: "And blessed is my God," he speaketh concerning his putting on the flesh of Adam. And again he speaketh concerning His putting on the flesh in Isaiah the Prophet, saying: "Who is this glorious One who cometh from Edom. Adonai, Who came down from heaven and put on the things of Bozrah, glorious in majesty?"[8]

When he saith "glorious" he refereth to His sweet odour; and when he saith "Adonai" he meaneth the Word of the Father Who was before the world was, the Son of God; and when he saith: "He put on the things of Bozrah, the glorious in majesty," he indicateth clearly the body of Adam.

Concerning Christians, David the Prophet prophesied, saying: "Declare ye to the nations that God is King and that He hath made firm the world so that it shall never be moved."[9] And concerning His coming to the nations, he said: "Before the face of God shall He come, He shall come

---

[1]Psalm 110:3   [2]Psalm 2:7   [3]Psalm 33:13
[4]Deuteronomy 32:43   [5]Psalm 132: 17-18   [6]Psalm 18:43-44
[7]Psalm 18: 45-46   [8]Isaiah 63:1   [9]Psalm 96:10

and shall judge the earth, and He shall judge the world in righteousness and the nations with justice."[1]

Thus Isaiah the Prophet prophesied and said: "The Lord of hosts shall destroy the evil of the nations, and He shall bring to nothing the nobles and the mighty ones of the earth."[2] Continuing his prophecy he said: "He shall come and shall build His house, and He shall deliver His people."[3]

Then he added these words, saying: "And at that time there shall spring from the root of Jesse, One Who shall reign over the nations, and the nations shall put their trust in Him and the place where He shall abide shall be glorious for ever."[4]

Again David prophesied, and said: "Sing ye unto God Who abides in Zion, and declare ye to the nations His work."[5]

Thus Solomon his son prophesied concerning our Saviour Emmanuel, the Sun of Righteousness, saying: "He brought me forth before the hills and established me before the world was, before He made the earth and the heavens. Before the floods of waters came forth and the beauty of the flowers appeared... and even before the winds blew, God created His work for his glory, and I existed along with My Father."[6]

And David his father again prophesied and said: "His name was before the sun, and before the moon, from generation to generation."[7]

Thus his son Solomon prophesied and said: "When He made strong the firmament above the clouds, and when He set in position the boundaries of the heavens... and when He set the sea in its appointed place, and before He founded His throne above the winds, and when He made strong the foundations of the earth... I existed along with Him."[8]

Then Ezekiel the Prophet prophesied and said: "The face of My God is in the East, and His light is brighter than the sun, and the nations put their trust in His Name."[9]

---

[1]Psalm 93:13; 98:9   [2]Isaiah 10:33; Haggai 2:7   [3]Isaiah 45:14; Haggai 2:7
[4]Isaiah 11:10   [5]Psalm 105:1-2   [6]Proverbs 8:22; John 1:1
[7]Psalm 72:5, 17   [8]Proverbs 8:30; John 1:1-3   [9]Ezekiel 43:2

Again Isaiah the Prophet prophesied and said: "Remember not the things of the past and think not about the things of olden time; behold I will make a new thing which shall now spring up, so that ye may know that I make a road through the desert and rivers of waters in the wilderness; and the beasts of the field shall follow after Me, also the young birds and the ostriches.

For I have given water in the desert, and made streams of water to flow in the wilderness, so that I may give to My people and to My chosen ones, that they may declare My glory and perform My commandment."[1]

Solomon prophesied and said of Him: "Who hath gone up into heaven and come down? And Who hath gathered together the winds in his bosom, and collected the waters in his hand, and the heavens on the palm of his hand? What is his name and what is the name of his son?"[2]

Thus Malachi the Prophet prophesied and said unto the Jews: "I have no pleasure in you, saith God Who ruleth all things. And I have no pleasure in your offerings, and I will accept no gift from your hands. For from the rising of the sun to its setting *shall My Name be praised among all peoples, and in all countries incense shall be offered up to My great Name, saith Almighty God."* [3]

Then Micah the Prophet prophesied saying: "A new covenant shall appear upon the mountain of God, and it shall be prepared upon the tops of the mountains, and it shall be exalted above the hills, and the people shall say: 'Come ye, let us go up into the mountain of God.' And many nations shall go there and they shall declare unto us His way, and we will walk therein."[4]

David he Prophet again prophesied and said: "Hearken unto Me O My people, and I will speak unto thee Israel, and will bring testimony to thee... I am God, thy God."[5]

---

[1]Isaiah 33:20; 35   [2]Micah 4:2; Compare Isaiah 2:3
[3]Malachi 1:10-11   [4]Micah 4:2; Compare Isaiah 2:3
[5]Psalm 50:7

Thus Moses the Prophet prophesied and said concerning the Godhead: "Hear, O Israel, the Lord thy God is One."[1] And this is to be explained thus; Father, and Son, and Holy Spirit are One God, Whose kingdom is one, Whose dominion is one, and as One shall men worship Them in the heavens and upon the earth, and in the depths of the seas. Unto Him be praise for ever and ever!

95. CHRIST'S GLORIOUS ENTRANCE INTO JERUSALEM

The prophets have prophesied concerning His glorious entrance into Jerusalem. Isaiah the Prophet said: "Shine thou, shine thou Jerusalem, thy light hath come and the glory of God hath risen upon thee."[2]

And the Prophet Zechariah prophesied saying: "Rejoice, rejoice daughter of Zion, and let Jerusalem shout for joy."[3]

And David prophesied and said: "Out of the mouth of children and babes Thou hast ordained strength because of the enemy, so that Thou mightest overthrow the enemy and the avenger."[4]

His son Solomon also prophesied and said: "The children are taught by God, and the peoples rejoice within thee."[5]

Again David his father prophesied and said: "Blow ye the horn in Zion on the day of the next moon, on the appointed day of our festival, for it is an ordinance for Israel."[6]

Then Ezra the Scribe prophesied and said: "Get ye out, make ye a festival in gladness and say unto the daughter of Zion, 'Rejoice thou, behold thy King hath come'."[7]

Isaiah, the Prophet prophesied and said: "Rejoice thou Jerusalem, rejoice thou. Behold, thy King hath come riding upon an ass. His reward is with Him, and His work is before His face."[8]

---

[1]Deuteronomy 6:4   [2]Isaiah 60:1   [3]Zechariah 9:9
[4]Psalm 8:2   [5]Isaiah 54:13   [6]Psalm 81:3
[7]Compare Zechariah 9:9   [8]Isaiah 52:11

Thus David the Prophet prophesied and said: "Blessed is He who cometh in the name of the Lord."[1]

Jacob the son of Isaac also prophesied and said: "Judah, thy brethren have praised thee, thy hand is upon the back of thine enemies and the children of thy mother shall worship thee. And the dominion shall not diminish from Judah, and the government shall not depart from his children, until he shall find Him Who hath been waited for, and Who is the Hope of the Nations."[2]

And he also prophesied and said: "His teeth are white as snow and His eyes are glad as with wine, and He shall wash His garments in wine and His tunic in the blood of clusters of grapes."[3] Again he prophesied and said: "Judah is a lion's cub; thou hast lain down and thou hast slept; no one shall wake him except him that hunteth until he findeth him; rise up from thy strong place."[4]

And Jacob blessed his son Judah, and said unto him: "There is a King who shall go forth from thee and shall wash His garments in wine, and glorious is the place of rest of the Beloved." By "Beloved" Christ is meant, and by "Messiah" Christ is meant, and Jesus meaneth "Saviour of the people." The prophets mention Christ under a secret name which interpreted means "the Beloved."

96. THE CRUCIFIXION

The Prophets also prophesied concerning the Crucifixion of Christ.

Moses, the servant of God, prophesied and said: "Ye shall see your salvation crucified upon the wood, and shall not believe."

David prophesied and said: "Many dogs have seized Me, and they drove nails through My hands and My feet; and they counted all my bones; and though they knew Me they despised Me, and they divided My garments among themselves and they cast lots for My apparel."[5]

---

[1]Psalm 118:26   [2]Genesis 49:8-10   [3]Genesis 49:11-12
[4]Genesis 49:9   [5]Psalm 22:16

Isaiah prophesied concerning the Incarnation and Crucifixion of Christ, and said: "Who believeth our word, and unto whom is the arm of the Lord revealed? And we spake as a child before Him; and He is like a root in parched ground, He hath no beauty and no form; and His form is more rejected and abased than that of any man. He is a broken man and a man of suffering; for He hath turned away His face, and they treat Him with contempt and esteem Him as nothing."[1]

Then he added these words, saying: "He hath taken our disease and carried our sickness, and by His wounds we are healed; and we saw Him suffering and wounded... and He opened not His mouth in His pain, and He came to be slaughtered; like a lamb before His shearer He opened not His mouth in His suffering until they took away His life and they knew not of His birth; through the sin of My people have I come even unto death."[2]

Jeremiah the Prophet prophesied and said: "And they took the price of the honourable one, thirty pieces of silver, he whom they had honoured among the Children of Israel. And God said unto me: 'Cast it into the melting pot, and test it and see if it be pure;' and they gave it to the potter's field. As God hath commanded me I will speak."[3]

Isaiah the Prophet prophesied and said: "They counted Him with the sinners, and brought Him to death."[4]

David the Prophet prophesied and said: "Those who hate me wrongfully are many, and they have rewarded Me with evil for good."[5]

Zechariah the Prophet prophesied and said: "And they shall look upon Him Whom they have crucified and pierced."[6]

And there are still many passages which have been written and many prophecies which might be mentioned concerning His coming, His Crucifixion, His death, His Resurrection and His second coming in glory.

---

[1]Isaiah 53:1-3   [2]Isaiah 53:4   [3]Zechariah 11:13
[4]Isaiah 53:12   [5]Psalm 35:12   [6]Zechariah 12:10

But we have only mentioned a few of those prophecies of the Prophets, so that ye may hear and believe, and understand, even as it is said in the Acts of the Apostles: "By the Gospel Thou hast guided us, and by the Prophets Thou hast comforted us; for the words of the Prophets make right the faith of those who doubt."[1]

97. THE RESURRECTION

David prophesied concerning His Resurrection and said: "I will arise, saith the Lord, and I will make salvation and manifest it openly."[2]

Again he saith: "Rise up, O Lord, and judge the earth, for thou shalt inherit among the nations."[3] He also prophesied and said: "Rise up, O Lord, help us and deliver us for Thy Name's sake."[4] And, "Let God arise and let His enemies be scattered, and let His enemies flee from before His face."[5]

Isaiah the Prophet prophesied and said: "He will remove sickness from His soul, for he hath not committed sin, and falsehood hath not been found in his mouth. And to him that hath served righteously and good, will he show light and he will justify him; and he shall do away with the sins of many, for he hath not committed sin and falsehood is not found in his mouth."[6]

Again David the Prophet prophesied and said: "For my soul shall not be left in hell."[7]

And Solomon his son prophesied and said: "The Sun of Righteousness shall arise and shall travel towards the right, and shall return into His place."[8]

---

[1]Acts 3:20 [2]Psalm 12:5 [3]Psalm 82:8

[4]Psalm 44:26 [5]Psalm 68:1 [6]Compare Isaiah 53:4

[7]Psalm 16:10 [8]Compare Malachi 4:2

98. THE ASCENSION OF CHRIST AND HIS SECOND COMING

All the prophets prophesied concerning His ascension and His second coming to judge the living and the dead.

David said concerning His Resurrection: "He hath gone up into the heights. Thou hast made captivity captive, and hast given grace unto the children of men."[1] And he also said: "Having gone forth, I will come back and I will return from the vastness of the sea."[2] And: "Sing ye unto God Who hath gone up into the heavens which are opposite the morning."[3]

Amos the Prophet also prophesied and said: "The Messiah, He Who made the time of the morning, hath come and is exalted from earth into the heights; and His name is God Who ruleth all things."[4]

Thus prophesied David the Prophet, saying: "Thou art exalted O Lord by Thy might, and we will praise and sing to Thy strength."[5]

Zechariah the Prophet prophesied and said: "His foot standeth on the Mount of Olives to the east of Jerusalem. And He rideth upon the Cherubim, and He flieth upon the wings of the wind."[6]

David said: "Open ye the gates of the princes and let the doors which were from the creation be opened, and the King of glory shall come! Who is the King of glory? God, the mighty and strong One, God, the mighty One in battle. The Lord God of Hosts is this King."[7]

Zechariah the Prophet prophesied and said: "On that day the Lord my God shall come, and all His saints with Him."[8] Again David the prophet prophesied and said: "God spake once, and this according to what I have heard: compassion belongeth to God. And Thine, O Lord, is the power, for Thou shalt reward every man according to his work."[9]

---

[1]Psalm 68:18   [2]Psalm 68:22   [3]Psalm 68:32-33
[4]Amos 4:13   [5]Psalm 21:13   [6]Zechariah 14:4; Psalm 18:10
[7]Psalm 24:7-8   [8]Zechariah 14:5   [9]Psalm 62:11-12

Then Daniel the Visionary prophesied and said: "I saw in my vision by night, and behold, there came one like unto the Son of man to the Ancient of Days, and there were given unto Him dominion, glory and sovereignty, and all the nations and peoples and countries shall serve Him, and His dominion shall have no end for ever and ever."[1]

And so, all the Prophets prophesied, and nothing hath happened without the prophecy of the Prophets. And they have declared everything that hath happened, and what shall happen, what hath been done and what shall be done, also that which belongeth to the times of old and that which belongeth to the latter days up to His second coming. All this they have done, not only by what they have prophesied and declared, but along with their prophecies they have given manifestations of Him in their bodies.[2]

When there was a famine in the land of Canaan and our father Abraham went down to Egypt, he came back with much riches and honour, and without blemish. In like manner our Redeemer went down and delivered the Church, the Assembly of the Nations, and He went up again, having gotten honour and praise.

99. THE PROPHETS AS FORERUNNERS OF CHRIST

Isaac rendered obedience unto his father, saying: "Bind Me;" and he was offered up as sacrifice, though he did not die, being redeemed by the ram which came down from heaven. In like manner the Son of God was obedient to His Father even unto death. And He was bound with His love for mankind, and He was nailed to the Cross and was pierced, and the Son of God became our ransom, but His Godhead suffered not.

Isaac's son Jacob departed to the land of Laban, the country of his mother's brother... he went with his staff only, and there he got much cattle, and acquired beasts both clean and unclean, and he fathered

---

[1] Daniel 7:13

[2] 'Stigmata': Marks resembling the wounds on the crucified body of Christ, believed to have been supernaturally impressed upon the bodies of certain saints.

twelve sons, and he revealed baptism, and returned to his own country where he received a blessing from Isaac his father.

In like manner our Lord Jesus Christ came down from heaven, the Word of God by Itself; and the staff of Jacob with which he pastured His sheep is our Lady Mary our salvation.

The staff represents the wood of the Cross, whereby, being crucified upon it, He redeemed his flock and took possession of us from among the Jews, the heathen and the Gentiles. And He chose for Himself twelve apostles who made the people in all the world and in every country to believe in Him, and He went up to heaven to His Father.

Thus Moses departed to the country of Midian, and there he held converse with God, Who made him to learn and to believe in the resurrection from the dead of his fathers Abraham, Isaac and Jacob. Then, by means of His rod, God gave unto him the power to perform miracles and he fathered two sons.

By this it is shown clearly that we shall be saved by the Godhead... for as the mouth of God proclaimed... "I am the God of Abraham" (meaning the Father),"and the God of Isaac" (meaning the Son), "and the God of Jacob" (meaning of the Holy Spirit), thus indicating the Trinity clearly and plainly: "I am not the God of the dead, but the God of the living,"[1] for they all are alive with God... and by this the resurrection of the dead is to be understood.

Jonah was swallowed up and cast into the belly of the great fish, and our Redeemer went down into the bowels of the earth, and rose again on the third day. Daniel was cast into the pit of the lions, and the king and his nobles sealed it with their seals, but he came out without the lions devouring him.

Similarly our Lord was cast into the grave, and the Jews sealed it with their seals, imagining that they were sealing up the rising of the sun so that it should not shine. O ye foolish, wicked, blasphemous, blind and

---

[1]Matthew 22:32

weak-minded men; would ye claim that the Spirit of Life should not appear and come forth? And the Jews were put to an open shame, and He went forth to shine upon us who have believed in Him.[1]

Joseph was sold into slavery by the hand of his brethren, and our Lord was sold by the hand of Judas. And Joseph, where he was sold, delivered his brethren from the famine, and Christ hath delivered us who believed in Him, and He hath made us His heirs and His brethren. And as Joseph gave an inheritance unto his brethren in the land of Goshen, so shall Christ give unto His righteous ones a habitation and an everlasting inheritance.

Moreover, in order that ye may know and understand, and be certain about the resurrection of the dead, I will give you a sign, which ye shall understand by the guidance of His word.

When Abraham had come unto the land of his inheritance, he bought first of all a tomb into which would be gathered together the dead bodies of his family, his children and his wife, so that he might join them in the resurrection; and there he buried his wife Sarah and he himself was buried there. For Abraham was a Prophet, and he knew that he would be raised up with his people. And Isaac and Rebekah his wife were also buried there.

And it remained their possession from the time when Jacob went down to the land of Egypt with seventy-seven souls (because of the famine and because Joseph his son was there), until their number became six hundred thousand marching men who were equipped for war, without reckoning women and children.

Jacob died in Egypt at a good old age, and he hath said unto Joseph his son: "I command thee by the life of my father and by my God, Who is the renewer of my life, that thou bury me not in this country, but in the tomb of my fathers, so that my death may be with them and my life subsequently also be with them."[2]

---

[1]Revelation 2:9; 3:9; John 15:22-25   [2]Genesis 47:29

And Joseph his son carried Israel (Jacob) and buried him by the grave of his fathers, for he reverenced the oath which Jacob had made him to swear.

When Jacob fell sick in Egypt, he called his brethren and his children, and made them to swear that they would not leave his bones in the land of Egypt, and said: "When God maketh you to return take ye my bones with you and mingle them in the grave of my fathers."[1]

100. THE CHARIOT AND THE VANQUISHER OF THE ENEMY

The Patriarchs then said unto Gregory, the Worker of Wonders: "Behold now, we know well, and thou hast made us to understand that *the Kings of Ethiopia have become glorious and great because of Zion. And the Kings of Rome also have become great because of the nails of the Cross that Queen Helena made into a bridle, and which hath become the vanquisher of the enemy.*

Now, tell us also how long shall the vanquisher of the enemy remain with the King of Rome… and the chariot carrying Zion with the King of Ethiopia. Tell us, for God hath revealed unto thee what hath been, and what shall be, vision and prophecy, like Moses and Elijah."

And Gregory answered and said unto them: "I will reveal unto you concerning the King of Rome, how he shall transgress the Covenant and trample the faith, provoking God to wrath.

This faith which we have ordered and laid down shall a king sitting in Rome transgress, and there shall be associated with him a certain Archbishop, and they shall change and pervert the word of God and cast it aside in the desire of their hearts, and they shall teach what they wish, and they shall change the Scriptures to suit their own nature, even as the Apostle saith: 'They have behaved themselves like the people of Sodom and Gomorrah.'[2] And our Lord said unto His disciples in the

---

[1]Genesis 50:25   [2]Matthew 10:15

Gospel, 'Guard ye yourselves against those who shall come unto you wearing the skin of sheep, and who are inwardly wolves that tear.'[1]

But when they have destroyed the faith, the vanquisher of the enemy shall be taken away from them, and none of these who have changed our faith shall sit upon the throne of Peter the Apostle; and the bowels of their Archbishops shall be emptied out if they have taken their seat upon it with their perverted faith. For the Angel of God, Uriel, hath been commanded to protect the throne of Peter in Rome. God Himself shall take away the vanquisher of the enemy from the king who shall not guard the faith, and the Persians shall make war upon him and shall defeat him.

And the King of Persia, whose name is Irenaeus, shall conquer him, and the king shall carry him away together with his horse, and by the Will of Almighty God the horse upon which is the vanquisher of the enemy shall be stirred up, and in a frenzy it shall go into the sea and perish there. But the nails of the bridle (the vanquisher of the enemy), shall shine there in the sea until Christ shall come again in great glory upon a cloud of heaven, with all His power and all His might.

This is what God showed me when I was in the pit. And now, concerning the King of Ethiopia and Zion the Bride of heaven, and her chariot upon which she moves, I will declare unto you that which my God hath revealed unto me and hath made me to understand. Ethiopia shall continue in the Christian faith until the coming of our Lord, and she shall in no way turn aside from the word of the Gospel, and it shall be so even as we have ordered until the end of the world."

Then one of the Patriarchs said unto Gregory, the Worker of Wonders and Miracles: "When Samalyal cometh, he who is the false Christ (the Antichrist), will the faith of the people of Ethiopia be destroyed by his attack?" And Gregory answered and said: "Surely not. David prophesied saying: 'Ethiopia shall make her hands come to God'."[2] And this that he saith meaneth that the Ethiopians will neither pervert nor change this our faith, nor the faith of those who were before us.

---

[1]Matthew 7:15   [2]Psalm 68:31

169

101. THE RETURN OF ZION

And the Tabernacle of the Law of God, the Holy Zion, shall remain in Ethiopia until that day when our Lord shall dwell on Mount Zion... and Zion shall come and shall appear unto all, prepared with three seals, even as Moses gave them unto her, and as it is written in the Old Law and in the New: "At the testimony of two or three witnesses everything shall stand."[1]

And then, at that time, saith Isaiah the Prophet: "The dead shall be raised up and those who are in the graves shall live, for the dew which cometh from Thee is their life."[2] *And when the dead are raised up, His mercy with which He waters the earth, shall cease; then they shall stand up before Him with the works which they have done.*

Enoch and Elias shall come, being alive, so that they may testify, and Moses and Aaron from the dead shall move around with everyone. And they shall open up Holy Zion, and they shall be seen by the Jews, the crucifiers, and they shall punish them and condemn them because of all they have done in perverting the Word of God.

And the Jews shall see what He wrote for them with His hand... the Words of His Commandments, and the manna with which He fed them in the wilderness without labour on their part, and the spiritual Zion which came down for their salvation, and the rod of Aaron which blossomed after the manner of Mary.

102. THE JUDGMENT OF ISRAEL

Then He shall say unto them: "Why did ye deny Me, and treated Me cruelly and crucified Me, seeing that I did all this for you, and that by My coming down from heaven I delivered you from the slavery of Satan, and that I came for your sake? Look ye and see how ye pierced Me with nails and thrust the spear through Me."

---

[1]Deuteronomy 19:15; Matthew 18:16; John 8:17   [2]Isaiah 26:19

And the twelve Apostles shall be risen up and they shall pass judgment upon them, and shall say unto them: "We would have made you hear, but ye would not hear the prophecy of the Prophets and the preaching of us the Apostles."

Then the Jews shall weep and repent when it shall be useless to do so, and they shall pass into everlasting punishment... and with the Devil their father who had directed them, and his demons who had led them astray, and with the wicked they shall be shut in.

And those who have believed and who have been baptized in His Holy Name, and have received His Body and His Blood, shall become His servants with their whole heart, for "there is no one who can hate his body altogether." The Body of Christ crieth out in our bodies, and He hath compassion because of His brethren.

If there are some who have sinned, they shall be judged in the fire according to the quantity of their sins; he whose burden of sin is light his punishment shall be light; and he whose burden of sins is heavy, exceedingly great shall his punishment be. One day with God is a period of ten thousand years; some there shall be who shall be punished for a day, and some for half a day; and some shall be tested and shall be absolved from their transgressions.

103. THE CHARIOT OF ETHIOPIA

Again the Patriarchs said unto Gregory, the Worker of Wonders and Miracles: "Behold now, thou hast told us concerning the vanquisher of the enemy of Rome, now tell us of the chariot of Ethiopia and whether it shall remain there up to the coming of Christ, as thou hast told us concerning Zion and the faith of the people of Ethiopia."

Then Gregory answered and said unto them: "It shall surely remain there. And again hearken ye unto me and I will declare this unto you; a few Jews shall lift up their heads against our faith in Nagran and in Armenia in the days after this; but this God will allow by His Will so that He may destroy them, for Armenia is a territory of Rome and Nagran is a territory of Ethiopia."

104. THE KING OF ROME AND THE KING OF ETHIOPIA

The King of Rome, the King of Ethiopia and the Archbishop of Alexandria were informed that they were to rise up to fight, to make war upon the enemies of God, the Jews, and they should destroy them.

The King of Rome, Enya, and the King of Ethiopia, Phinehas, were to lay waste their lands and build churches there, and they were to cut to pieces all Jews at the end of this Cycle in twelve cycles of the moon. Then the kingdom of the Jews shall be made an end of, and the Kingdom of Christ shall be constituted until the advent of the False Messiah.

Afterward two other kings, Justinus the King of Rome and Kaleb the King of Ethiopia, met together in Jerusalem where their Archbishop was to make offerings, and they were to establish the Faith in love, and give each other gifts and the salutation of peace, then they were to divide between them the rulership of the earth, from the centre of Jerusalem, as we have already stated.[1]

Also for love's sake and in brotherhood they were to have jointly the royal title of King of Ethiopia. They were both to be mingled with David and Solomon their fathers. The one whom they chose to be named King of Rome was also to be called "King of Ethiopia," and the King of Ethiopia likewise was to bear the name of "King of Rome," and they were to have part in the inheritance whereby they should be named with David and Solomon their fathers.

And thus after they had become united in a common bond and had established the right faith, they were to determine that the Jews were no longer to live, and each of them was to leave his son there in Jerusalem; and the King of Ethiopia was to leave there his firstborn son whose name was Israel, and was to return to his own country in joy.

Then, when he came to his royal house, he was to give abundant thanks unto God and offer up his body as an offering of praise to his God. And

---

[1]See Part I, Chapter 18

God shall accept him gladly, for he shall not defile his body after he hath returned, but he shall go into spiritual seclusion in purity of heart.

He shall then make king his youngest son, whose name is Gabra Maskal, and he shall shut himself up in a monastery. When this hath been told to the king of Nagran, the son of Kaleb, he shall come in order to reign over Zion, and Gabra Maskal shall make his armies to rise up in arms, and he shall journey in a chariot and they shall meet together at the narrow end of the Sea of Liba, and shall fight together.

On that same night the two of them shall pray from sunset until the dawn of day, when the battle shall be raging strong upon them. And when they have cried out to Him with tears, God will consider the prayer of both of them, and the penitent prayers of their father, and will say: "This one is the elder and he hath stood up to perform the will of his father, and that one, the younger, hath loved his father and hath prayed to God for him."

Then God will say to Gabra Maskal: "Choose thou between the chariot and Zion," and He will cause him to take Zion, and he shall reign openly upon the throne of his father. And God will make Israel (the eldest son of the King of Ethiopia) to choose the chariot, and he shall reign secretly and he shall not be visible, and He will send him to all those who have transgressed the commandment of God.

No one shall build houses and none shall suffer fatigue in labouring nor suffer thirst on the journey, and they shall live in tents. And their days shall be double those of ordinary men, and they shall use bows and arrows and shall shoot at and pierce him that God hateth.

Thus hath *God made for the King of Ethiopia more glory, grace and majesty than for all the other things of the earth because of the greatness of Zion, the Tabernacle of the Law of God, the heavenly Zion.*

May God make us to perform His spiritual good pleasure, and deliver us from His wrath, and make us to share His kingdom.

Then they answered and said unto him: "Verily, thou hast spoken well, for thus was it revealed unto thee by the help of the Holy Spirit. Thou hast told us everything which hath taken place, and thou art in agreement with the book of Domitius of Rome.

Thou hast prophesied also what shall happen to the two cities, the brides of Christ, Rome and Ethiopia, the great cities of God, and to the churches in Nestasya, Arkadya, Marena and Armenia, where pure sacrifices and offerings shall be offered up at all times."

May God show us His grace. Christ is our King, and in Christ is our life for ever and ever. Amen.

APPENDIX I

ETHIOPIA (ABYSSINIA) A Brief Historical Synopsis

Area: 1,221,900 square kilometres.

Population: 27,000,000 (approx.)

Capital: Addis Ababa ("new flower")

Languages: Almost 100 distinct languages plus several dialects: Principal languages are Amharic, Tigrinya, Gurage. Geez, the language of the ancient Aksumite empire survives as a literary and liturgical language and is now called Ethiopic.

Economy: Based almost exclusively on agriculture.

Ethiopia has had a continuous existence as a nation for over two thousand years, and during most of this time its contact with the rest of the world has been minimal. Known in antiquity as Punt or the "Land of God," Ethiopia has been able to preserve a rich and unique culture, mainly because of its geographic isolation, and the fact that it was the sole black African country to maintain its independence against foreign encroachments.

Christianity has been, and still is, the dominant religion, and was introduced in the 4th century, making Ethiopia the oldest Christian nation on earth. Islam was introduced in the 7th century.

Jewish influence penetrated Ethiopia during the era of the Aksum Kingdom and left an important mark on the nation's religious customs. A remnant of these converts persists to this day in the "Falashas" of Northern Ethiopia whose preservation of, and adherence to, Old Testament Jewish traditions is undeniable, for they observe the Sabbath, practise circumcision, have synagogue services, follow certain dietary laws of Judaism, observe many laws of ritual cleanliness, offer sacrifices on Nisan 14 in the Jewish religious year, and observe the major Jewish festivals. They were first discovered by Joseph Halevy in 1867 and number around 20,000 living mostly in the regions north of Lake Tana, generally remaining aloof from other Ethiopians. They call themselves Beta Israel (House of Israel), though they know no Hebrew and are of local ethnic stock.

Attempts by the Portuguese who were seeking the legendary Christian Kingdom of the monarch Prester (Priest) John and by the notorious Jesuits, to convert the country to Roman Catholicism, led to serious conflicts culminating in the expulsion of the Jesuits in 1633.

The Solomonic Restoration

Late in the 13th century, the Zagwe usurpers of the throne were swept away, and **Yekuno Amlak (ruled 1270-1285)** restored the Solomonic dynasty of Kings, legitimate heirs of the Aksumite line as defined by the traditions of the KEBRA NAGAST.

Theodore II (ruled 1855-1868): As a consequence of the two-year delay by Queen Victoria of England in replying to a letter that the emperor had sent, several British officials were imprisoned at Magdala. In July 1867 a British military force, led by Robert Napier was dispatched to Ethiopia to secure the release of the Englishmen. After courageous resistance, the last mountain fortress was captured in April 1868, and Emperor Theodore committed suicide to avoid capture.

In **1889 Menyelek II** ascended the throne, and in March 1896 he inflicted a crushing defeat on the invading Italian forces. Menyelek died in December 1913, and his successor, the Muslim adherent Lij Yasu was forcefully dethroned, and Menyelek's daughter Empress Zauditu was crowned, with Ras Tafari, son of Menyelek's cousin Ras Makonnen as Regent and heir to the throne.

In **1928 Ras Tafari** was crowned Negus (King) and two years later on November 2, 1930, following the death of Empress Zauditu, he was crowned Emperor of Ethiopia and took the name Haile Selassie I (Power of the Holy Trinity) and the inherited Solomonic titles, "King of Kings, Lord of Lords, Elect of God, Conquering Lion of the tribe of Judah," he being the 225th rebirth of Solomon and direct descendant of the union of King Solomon with the Queen of Sheba.

Much credit is given to this last ruler of the Solomonic line of Kings for the modernization of the imperial realm, the issuing of a Constitution, the active role of Ethiopia in world affairs within a policy of peaceful neutrality, and the general improvement of living conditions for the people.

The rapacious invasion and occupation of Ethiopia by fascist Italian forces in 1935 evidenced the impotence of the League of Nations to protect its weaker members. Ethiopia resisted for seven months until Addis Ababa fell on May 5, 1936. But certain regions of Ethiopia were never conquered. This unprovoked attack which was blessed by the Roman Pontiff as a "Catholic Crusade," was particularly cruel in its execution. The Italians murdered Archbishop Petros (the Coptic abuna) and massacred the monks of the great monastery of Debre Libanos, and after an attempted coup, decimated the population of Addis Ababa during a three-day frenzied orgy of murder and pillage in February 1937. With British and French help, Ethiopia was delivered from the Italian invasion, and Emperor Haile Selassie returned to its liberated capital on May 5, 1941. A renewal of relations with the papacy, broken off since 1632, was approved in June 1969 culminating in a visit by the Emperor to the Vatican on November 9, 1970.

In 1974 the abolition of the monarchy in Ethiopia was proclaimed by the tyrannical Moscow-backed Marxist-Communist Derg government, after the overthrow of the Emperor and the Ethiopian Royal Solomonic Dynasty, and the imprisonment of the imperial family.

There was throughout Ethiopia, widespread resistance by the people to the communist policies of forced slave labour in remote areas, resulting in soil degradation, famine, and general impoverishment of the nation. Eventually, the Communist government was overthrown, and today Ethiopia is on the verge of determining its political future, including the settlement of the thorny Eritrean issue.

Many patriotic organizations established by exiled Ethiopians in various countries, are struggling for a re-establishment of the monarchy and the Royal Dynasty based on ancient traditions of the KEBRA NAGAST.

APPENDIX II

THE FALASHAS

The world marvelled once more at the extraordinary skill and military genius displayed by the state of Israel, in rescuing thousands of Ethiopian Jews from the famine that was ravaging the land of the Negus in 1984.

Under the "Law of Return" which gives every Jew the right to full Israeli citizenship, vast numbers of immigrants have entered Israel. Among these have been some 100,000 survivors of the Nazi death camps. "Operation Magic Carpet" brought in thousands of Jews from Yemen and Morocco, and some 120,000 more were flown in from Iraq in "Operation Ezra and Nehemiah"; but it was not until February of 1980 that the mission of rescuing the Falashas was entrusted to Israel's famed and highly efficient intelligence agency, the Mossad.

In a major secret operation, Israeli agents rounded up tens of thousands of these ostracized people and led them across deserts and mountains into Sudan, where border camps were prepared to receive them, and specially chartered planes would take them 'on wings of Eagles' to Zion, to the Promised Land, to Israel.

Who were these peoples? What impelled the Israeli authorities to undertake such a vast and costly enterprise shrouded in secrecy and hidden even from their own population?

In modern Ethiopia live a number of people, estimated at some twenty-three thousand. They are a remarkable people indeed: black-skinned, but with strong Jewish ties. In Ethiopia they are known as "Falashas" meaning stranger or outsider.

For many centuries the existence of Falashas, or "Black Jews", was unknown to the outside world. All knowledge about them had been lost. It was only in the nineteenth century that they were rediscovered by missionaries and anthropologists. Since then their history has been painstakingly reconstructed and their religion assiduously studied. Many surprising conclusions were made, but baffling mysteries remain.

The Falashas' religious ties to the service of Jehovah are obvious, and it appears that their religious development had its beginnings long ago because they knew nothing of the Talmud, a body of writings that reflected relatively late developments of Jewish religious thoughts and philosophy.

The Falashas, the Jews of Ethiopia, call themselves "Beta Israel" (House of Israel), and according to their traditions, they originated from the nobles of Jerusalem who accompanied Menyelek (David II), (the son of King Solomon and Makeda, Queen of Sheba) when he returned to his country. Another opinion holds that the Falashas were descendants of Jewish soldiers who in ancient times manned the south border garrisons of Egypt. Finally, some believe that the Falashas are merely a segment of a local population which at one time in the past converted to Judaism. Thus the mystery of their origin has not been entirely solved. According to scientific theories, they are of Hamltlc (Cushite) origin and belong to the Agau family of tribes which already formed part of the Ethiopian population prior to the settlement of the Semitic tribes who arrived from southern Arabia.

Ethiopian chronicles show that Judaism was widespread before the conversion to Christianity of the Aksum dynasty during the fourth century. After this, those who remained faithful to Judaism were persecuted and compelled to retreat from the coastal region into the mountains north of Lake Tana. They concentrated themselves in this region and lived in political independence under their own rulers.

The Falashas played an active role in the uprising of the Agau tribes against the Aksum dynasty in the tenth century. According to Ethiopian tradition, there was a Jewish queen known as Judith (or Esther) who led the rebels in deposing the Negus and vented their anger against the Christians, their churches and their monasteries. Thus began a sporadic war between Christians, Jews and Muslims with the eventual defeat of the Falashas by the Negus Ishaq in the early fifteenth century. Later, it was the Negus Zara Yakob (1434-1468) who gave himself the title of "Exterminator of the Jews", and his son Baeda Maryam (1468-1478) organized a massacre of the Falashas. Paradoxically, Ethiopian chronicles praise their bravery and their devotion to their religion.

In spite of the massive Falasha losses in these wars, the strength of the Falashas was not completely broken, so when the Agau tribes again rose in rebellion during the reign of the Negus Susenyos (1607-1632), the Falashas, under the leadership of their king, Gideon, participated in the revolt.

However, after the Negus had subdued the other rebels, he directed the whole of his power against the Falashas, and he conquered their fortresses. Men, women and children were killed.

The Negus then promised the remaining Falashas that they could return in peace to their villages if they laid down their arms. After a short while, however, the Negus reneged on his promise, and presented them with the alternative of conversion or death.

In the great massacre perpetrated against those who refused to accept baptism, King Gideon lost his life. Thereafter, many Falashas were sold as slaves, and the death penalty was decreed against those who continued to observe Jewish customs. These events marked the end of Falasha independence. Even their lands were confiscated, and they were compelled to till them as tenants.

In the course of time they were permitted to return to their former religion; and even though there were no further wars, from then on suffering and degradation were the lot of the Falashas. In spite of all this, the Falashas retained their distinctiveness, and considered themselves part of the Jewish people, both in their origin and faith.

Their religion is based on the Bible, which they possess in the Geez language in the same translation as that adopted by the Ethiopian Church; it includes a number of Apocryphal books (Tobit, Judith, Wisdom of Solomon, Wisdom of Ben Sira, I and II Maccabees, and the Book of Baruch). In addition to these they consider the books of Enoch and Jubilees sacred texts. The Falashas have priests who claim descent from Aaron, and in every region they inhabit, the priests elect a High Priest who then becomes the spiritual leader of the community.

The sanctity of the Sabbath is rigorously observed by the Falashas. Work ceases on Friday at midday when all purify themselves by ritual immersion and the wearing of their Sabbath clothes. The lighting of candles or the kindling of fire, the drawing of water, going beyond the limits of the village, and sexual intercourse are forbidden on the Sabbath. From Ethiopian sources it also appears that in ancient times the Falashas observed the Sabbath rest even when in war, and fought only when attacked.

The Falashas determine their festivals by means of a calendar patterned after the Jewish one, and they celebrate the new moons and the Jewish festivals as prescribed in the Pentateuch. Their adherence to the practice of male circumcision performed on the eighth day after birth as is prescribed biblically, further confirms their Jewish religious ancestry.

The laws of ritual uncleanness and purity receive special attention by the Falashas. Their wives stay in a special hut on the outskirts of the village during the days of their menstruation and they return to their homes only after having purified themselves by immersion. A special hut is also prepared for women in confinement. The uncleanness lasts for forty days if a male child is born, and eighty days if it is a female child. Upon the conclusion of her days of uncleanness, the woman shaves off the hair of her head, immerses herself, and washes her clothes before returning to her home. The confinement hut is then burned down.

The Falashas do not eat raw meat like other Ethiopians, and they observe the Pentateuchal laws concerning the ritually clean and unclean animals and the purging of the sinew of the femoral vein. For this reason the Falashas do not eat meat slaughtered by Christians. Family life is usually exemplary. Divorce is rare and only adultery is recognized as a justification for it. It is for this reason that the Falashas are not affected by the venereal diseases which are so widespread in Ethiopia.

The Falashas firmly believe in only one God, the God of Israel, who has chosen His people and Who will send the Messiah to redeem them and return them to the Holy Land. On several occasions prophets arose among the Falashas who announced the coming of the Messiah and caused messianic movements to emerge. During the reign of Emperor Theodore II, in 1862, such an episode was responsible for the disaster which overtook a large group of Palashas who attempted to reach Israel by foot. Most of them died on the way and the remainder returned, broken and destitute.

The Falashas believe in the World to Come and the Resurrection of the Dead. In their writings there are detailed descriptions of the rewards which await the righteous in the Garden of Eden and the chastisements and punishments which await the wicked. Edward Ullendorf, noted authority on the traditions and culture of the Falashas, saw in their Judaism a strange fusion of pagan, Jewish and Christian beliefs and practices. On the other hand, Joseph Halevy and other researchers were deeply impressed by their Jewish consciousness.

Today most of the Falashas speak Amharic, which is the official language of Ethiopia. Their literature, however, is written entirely in Geez, the classical Ethiopian language which is to this day the holy language of the Ethiopian Church. The Bible is read also in the same Geez. It is a translation which was made not from the original Hebrew text but from the Septuagint. This is also the translation accepted by the Ethiopian Church, and there is no evidence as to whether the Falashas ever possessed a different version which was closer to the original.

The Portuguese Jesuits of the 17th century asserted that in their days the Falashas possessed the Bible in Hebrew and knew a faulty Hebrew. According to one tradition, the last king of the Falashas (during the reign of the Negus Susenyos) burnt their books before his death; but another tradition, reported by Filosseno Luzzatto, says that the Falashas hid all their Hebrew books in the town of Gondar so that they would not fall into the hands of their enemies. In all these tales there is difficulty in distinguishing fact from legend.

The book Teezaza Sanbat (Precepts of the Sabbath) is an original Falasha work, and they attribute it to Aba Zabra, a monk who lived in the days of the Negus Zara Yakob (15th century). It is a collection of the laws of the Sabbath (according to the Book of Jubilees) and of legends on the creation of man, the Garden of Eden, Noah, Abraham, Moses and others. This work does not exist in a Christian version, but some parts of it have been introduced, with slight changes, into a Christian work entitled Dersana Sanbat (The Sermon on the Sabbath), which praises the so-called "Christian Sabbath", that is, Sunday.

In addition to these works, there are also texts which have not yet been published, such as those in the Faitlovitch Library in Tel Aviv, Israel, and which include such works as "The Testament of Isaac", "The Testament of Jacob", "The Praises of Wisdom", "The Words of Moses" and others. It may be assumed that there are still more unknown works in other libraries and in the hands of the Falashas. It appears that all the books of the Falashas were written before the loss of their independence.

Mention has already been made of the tradition on the origin of the Falashas from the Jews who accompanied Menyelek, the son of King Solomon and the Queen of Sheba, when he returned from Jerusalem to Ethiopia. Since the Ethiopians themselves, especially the royal dynasty, claim the same origin, the Falashas added a story: on his way Menyelek crossed a river on the Sabbath with the Holy Ark of the Covenant which he had stolen from the temple in Jerusalem. Some of his followers crossed over with him and from that time he and his sinful companions became Christians, while the other followers who observed the Sabbath became the fathers of the Falashas.

The story contends that the Holy Ark was indeed deposited in Aksum, within a secret cave which was subsequently sealed after an earthquake caused a landslide. It is only when a Falasha approaches it that the wall is opened up and remains thus until he has prostrated himself before the Holy Ark.

It is estimated that there are approximately some 12,000 Falashas still living in the area north of Lake Tana and in the outskirts of the town of Gondar. They are mainly engaged in agriculture, but as previously mentioned, they do not own their own land. Therefore, working as lessees or tenants on the land, they must hand over the major part of their produce to the landowners. In addition to this, the Falashas (both men and women) engage in various crafts such as pottery, weaving, basketry, spinning, and work as blacksmiths and goldsmiths.

Ever since their modern day "discovery" by Joseph Halevy in 1867, the Falashas have been the subject of unending fascination and study by a variety of scholars. The abundance of legends and traditions that permeate their history, has also fueled much speculation as to their true origins and ancestry.

In general, the outward appearance of the Falasha is similar to that of the Amhara. As a result of the intermingling of Hamitic and Semitic bloods, there are differences in the coloring of the skin and the facial features, which at times tend towards the Agau type and at others toward the Semitic type found in Oriental Jews. However, an anthropological study has not yet been carried out.

The question of how Jewish the Falashas are, or whether they are indeed Jews at all, is still very much a matter of considerable debate in Israel. Although some of the Hasidic Jews and other orthodox groups both in Israel and in the United States, still refuse to recognize them as Jews in any sense, their dramatic rescue in the secretive "Operation Moses", has provided adequate proof that the State of Israel regards them as Jews.

There are a number of theories connecting the Falashas with the Israelites of old. Some claim that when the Hebrews left Egypt at the time of the Biblical Exodus, a group broke off from the rest and found their way south to Ethiopia, where they eventually established their own kingdom. However, one of the most popular and persistent beliefs is that the Falashas are one of the "lost ten tribes of Israel."

Around the year 964 B.C. after the death of King Solomon, a breakaway took place in Israel. Ten of the twelve tribes seceded and under Jeroboam, formed the Northern Kingdom. Then, when this Northern Kingdom fell to the brutal Assyrian army some 200 years later, the majority of the Israelites were forcibly deported to Assyria where they lost their separate identity and were assimilated. Many orthodox Jews believe that the Falashas are the lost tribe of Dan. However, this notion has no historical basis. The important question is not where did the Falashas come from, but rather, where did their Jewish religion come from.

Regardless of the true nature of their origin or conversion to Judaism, the fact remains that the Falashas constitute a living testimony to the exciting saga of the transfer of the Ark of the Covenant from the temple in Jerusalem to a still unknown location in Ethiopia.

The numerous prophecies in Daniel, chapters 8, 9 and 11 concerning the restoration of the temple in Jerusalem, the "daily sacrifice", and the many predictions as to the rediscovery of the Ark of God and its return to God's temple, makes the emergence of the Falasha Jews of Ethiopia an event of undeniable prophetic importance.

It is known that at present in Israel an intense training of young Levite youths in the priestly rituals of temple ceremonials is taking place, with a view to an early establishment of the Biblical system of sacrificial worship. The presence of thousands of Falashas in Israel, themselves the only living descendants of the custodians of God's Holy Ark of the Covenant, may in fact signal the start of a series of prophetic events culminating with the rebuilding of the Temple of God in Jerusalem, and the return of the Messiah as King.

Ethiopia, the Biblical land of the "men with the burnt faces" is yet to fulfill its greatest prophetic destiny, and the Falasha Jews are at the centre of these coming earth-shaking events.

M.F.B.

BIBLIOGRAHPY

KEBRA NAGAST (The Glory of Kings)

Select bibliography and recommended reading:

Arberry, A.J. *Religion in theMiddle East* (1969).

Archer, G.L. *Encyclopaedia of Bible Difficulties* (Grand Rapids, Zondervan, 1982).

Baron, S.W. *Social and Religious History of the Jews* (1952).

Barr, James. *The Semantics of Biblical Language* (London, Oxford University Press, 1961).

Blackman, E.C. *Biblical Interpretation* (Philadelphia, Westminster Press, 1957).

Bliss, S. *Analysis of Sacred Chronology* (Oakland, Calif. Pacific Press, 1887).

Bouton, S.W and Doane T.W. *Bible Myths* (1928)

Braden, Charles S. *Spirits in Rebellion* (Dallas, Southem Methodist University Press, 1963).

Brooks, J. W. *Elements of Prophetical Interpretation* (Philadelphia, Orin Rogers, 1841).

Bruce, F. *The Books and the Parchment,* Some chapters on the Transmission of the Bible (Fleming H. Revell Co., 1953).

Bruce, James. *Travels to discover the source of the Nile,* 3rd edition (7 vols, 1813).

Bryant, T.A. *Today's Dictionary of the Bible* (Bethany House, 1982).

Budge, E.A.W. *Annals of the Nubian Kings* (London, n.d.).

Budge, E.A.W. *The Queen of Sheba and her son Menyelek* (London n.d.).

Casely-Hayford, J.E. *Ethiopia Unbound* (Accra, Ghana, 1911).

Colbi, S.P. *Christianity in the Holy Land, Past and Present* (1969).

Coleman, B. *Constantine The Great and Christianity* (New York, Columbia University Press, 1914).

Comay, J. *The Temple of Jerusalem* (New York, 1957).

Coudenhove-Calergy, H. *Anti-Semitism through the ages* (1935).

Dowling, John. *The History of Romanism, From the Earliest Corruptions of Christianity* (New York, Edward Walker, 1871).

Ehrman, Dr. Esther J., and Levine, Moshe. *The Tabernacle; Melechet Hamishkan* (Tel Aviv, Israel, 1969).

Eliodoro de Reina, Cipriano de Valera. *La Santa Biblia* (1901).

Ferguson, Charles. *New Books of Revelation* (Garden City, N.J., Doubleday-Doran, 1929).

Flannery, E.H. *Anguish of the Jews* (1965).

Forlong, J.G.R. *Encyclopaedia of Religions* (New Hyde Park, New York, University Books, 1964).

Free, Joseph R. *Archaeology and Bible History* (Wheaton, Ill. Van Kampen Press, 1950).

Goldberg, B.Z. *The Sacred Fire* (New York, Liveright, 1930).

Gutmann, J. *The Temple of Solomon* (Missoula, 1976).

Hacker, *The Cross: Its History and Symbolism* (1934).

Hahn, Herbert F. *The Old Testament in Modern Research* (Philadelphia, Fortress Press, 1966).

Haran, Menahem. *The Ark and The Cherubim: Their Symbolic Significance in Biblical Ritual* (Israel Exploration Journal, 1959).

Hay, M. *The Foot of Pride; The Pressure of Christendom on the People of Israel for 1900 years* (1950).

Hislop, Alexander. *The Two Babylons* (New York, Loizeaux Brothers, 1959 ed. First publication, 1853).

Hirn, Yrjo. *The Sacred Shrine* (London; Macmillan & Co., 1912).

Jackson, Howard M. *The Lion Becomes Man: The Leontomorphic Creator* (Ph.D. dissertation; Claremont Graduate School, 1983).

Jamieson, Fausset, Brown. *Commentary on the Whole Bible* (Zondervan Pub. House, 1961).

Jamison, T.H. *A Prophet Among You,* n.d. (Pacific Press).

Josephus, Flavius. *Antiquities of the Jews* (Philadelphia, John C. Winston, Co., 1957 ed).

Kalisch, Dr. Isador (translator). *Sepher Yezirah, A Book on Creation or the Jewish Metaphysics of Remote Antiquity* (Rosicrucian Press, 1966).

Kaufman, Y. *The Religion of Israel* (1960).

Koester, Helmut. *Apocryphal and Canonical Gospels* (Harvard Theological Review #73, 1980).

Leslau, Wolf. *Falasha Anthology: The Black Jews of Ethiopia* (New York, Shocken, 1969).

Lewis, Spencer. *The Secret Doctrines of Jesus* (Rosicrucian Press, 1965).

Littman, Dr. E. *The Legend of the Queen of Sheba in the Tradition of Aksum* (Leyden, 1904).

Malan, G. *Book of Adam and Eve* (London, 1882).

Martin, Walter. *The Kingdom of the Cults* (Bethany House Publishers, 1965).

Mason, Ruth. *A People in Anguish* (In the Jewish Monthly, vol. 102 No. 4).

Mead, Dodd. *Strange Sects and Curious Cults* (New York, 1961).

Meyer, Marvin W. *The Secret Teachings of Jesus* (New York, Vintage Books, 1984).

Neuser, J. *History of the Jews in Babylonia* (5 vols., 1965-1970).

Newton, Thomas. *Dissertations on the Prophecies* (London, Rivington, 1804).

Orlinsky, H. *Ancient Israel* (1954) .

Parfitt and Kessler. *The Falashas*; Minority Rights Group Report No. 67 (London, 1985).

Parfitt, Dr. Tudor. *Operation Moses* (Exodus of the Falasha Jews from Ethiopia) (1985).

Perkins, Pheme. *Journal of Biblical Literature #101 'On Johannine Traditions'* (1982).

Pritchard, James B. *Ancient Near Eastern Texts* (Princeton University Press, 1955).

Rappoport, L. *The Lost Jews. Last of the Ethiopian Falashas* (New York, Stein and Day, 1980).

Robinson & Koester. *Trajectories through Early Christianity* (Philadelphia, Fortress, 1971).

Robinson & Meyer (ed.) *The Nag Hammadi Library in English* (Leiden, Brill, 1977).

Rolef, Susan Hattis. *Political Dictionary of the State of Israel* (1987).

Rossini, Carlo-Conti. *Etiopia e genti d' Etiopia* (Rome, 1937) .

Rossini, Conti. *Records of a Sojourn in Eritrea* (Asmara, 1903, translated from the Italian).

Russell, Letty M. *The Liberating Word* (Philadelphia, Westminster, 1976).

Schoeps, Hans-Joachim. *Jewish Christianity* (Philadelphia, Fortress, 1969).

Smith, Ethan. *View of the Hebrews* (Smith & Shute, 1823).

Smith, Homer W. *Man and His Gods* (Boston, Little, Brown & Co, 1953).

Smith, Oswald J. *Who are the False Prophets?* (Toronto, The People's Press).

Smith, Uriah. *Daniel and the Revelation* (Review and Herald, 1944).

Sokolow, N. *History of Zionism* (1918).

Stern, H.A. *Wanderings Among the Falashas in Abyssinia* (1862, 1968).

Strong, J. *The Tabernacle of Israel in the Desert* (Grand Rapid, 1952).

Takoma Park, M.D. *Problems in Bible Translation* (General Conference Seventh Day Adventists).

Thompson, D.D., Ph.D. F.C. *The Thompson Chain-Reference Bible.*

Tuchman, B. *Bible and Sword* (1956).

Ullendorf, Edward. *Ethiopia and the Bible* (Oxford University Press, London, 1968).

Unger, Merril. *Archaeology and the Old Testament* (Zondervan Pub. House, 1966).

Van Baalen, J.K. *Chaos of the Cults* (Grand Rapids, W.B. Erdmans Publ. Co 1962).

Van Vorst, Mrs. J. *Magda, Queen of Sheba* (8 vols., New York, London, 1907, translated from the French).

Walsh, Mary E. *The Wine of Roman Babylon* (Nashville, Southern Pub. Assoc., 1945).

Wansbrough, Henry (ed.). *The New Jerusalem Bible* (New York, Doubleday, 1985).

Weigall, Arthur. *The Paganism in our Christianity* (New York, Putnam & Son, 1928).

Weisbord, R.G. *African Zion* (1966).

Wilhelm, K. *Roads to Zion* (1948).

Wilson, Robert D. *A Scientific Investigation of the Old Testament* (Philadelphia, n.d.).

Wisse, Frederik. *The Interpreter's Dictionary of the Bible* (Nashville, Abingdon, 1976).

Woodrow, Ralph. *Babylon Mystery Religion, Ancient and Modern* (1966).

Wright, Prof. W. *Catalogue of Ethiopia Manuscripts at British Museum* (London, The Makdala Collection, n.d.).

Young, E.J. *An Introduction to the Old Testament* (W.B. Eerdmans Pub. Co., 1958).

Zodhiates, Th.D., Dr. Spiro. *The Hebrew-Greek Study Bible* (AMG International, 1988).

****

Bulletin of the School of Oriental and African Studies (University of London, No. 24, 1961).

Facsimile Edition of the Nag Hammadi Codices (Dept of Antiquities, Arab Republic of Egypt, 1972).

Myth, Legend and Custom in the Old Testament (New York, Harper and Row, 1969).

Strong's Exhaustive Concordance of the Bible (New York, Abindgon-Cokesbury Press).

The Legacy of Rome (Oxford, The Clarendon Press, 1923).

Dr Miguel F. Brooks

ABOUT THE TRANSLATOR/EDITOR

Dr Miguel F. Brooks is a teacher, author-publisher, biblical scholar and researcher. Born in Panama of Jamaican parents, he received his early training in sciences, literature, philosophy and medicine. A graduate of the Instituto Istmeño in Panamá and Universidad de Carabobo in Venezuela, he is a member of several academic and philosophic societies and holds a B.Sc. degree in General Sciences and a Ph.D. in Psychology.

A trained interpreter and translator (English, Spanish, Portuguese), Dr Brooks is an ordained elder and lay preacher in the Seventh-Day Adventist Church, and is currently engaged in biblical and historical research in prophetic inter-pretation and Old Testament exegesis.